COMPUTER CONSCIOUSNESS: SURVIVING THE AUTOMATED 80s

H. Dominic Covvey

TORONTO GENERAL HOSPITAL
TORONTO, ONTARIO, CANADA

Neil Harding McAlister

TORONTO GENERAL HOSPITAL
TORONTO, ONTARIO, CANADA

ADDISON-WESLEY PUBLISHING COMPANY

Reading, Massachusetts • Menlo Park, California
London • Amsterdam • Don Mills, Ontario • Sydney

This book is in the
Addison-Wesley Series
Joy of Computing

Consulting Editor
T. A. Dwyer

Library of Congress Cataloging in Publication Data

Covvey, H. Dominic.
   Computer consciousness.

   (The Joy of computing series)
   Includes bibliographical references and index.
   I. Computers.   I. McAlister, Neil Harding,
1952–   joint author.   II. Title.   III. Series:
Joy of computing series
QA76.C64   001.64   79-27144
ISBN 0-201-01939-6

ISBN 0-201-01939-6
     DEFGHIJ-AL-8987654321

This book is dedicated to
Bill Gruener, Mary Clare McEwing,
and Debbie Schreiber . . . without whom, nothing!

Foreword

By 1984, computer systems will in each year record thousands of details on the activities of every individual. By 1984, computer systems may transfer funds automatically from a consumer's bank account as soon as he or she makes a purchase. By 1984, many assembly lines will be almost totally automated, with only a few residual employees remaining to monitor the machines. By 1984, many businesses with five or more employees will manage their finances and produce their documents with the aid of computers. By 1984, many working professionals — doctors, lawyers, accountants, architects, scientists, engineers — will be using computers to enhance their creativity and productivity in daily work. By 1984, stories in most North American newspapers will have been typed into a computer, edited with the aid of a computer, and typeset by a computer program. By 1984, many upper middle class and upper class homes in North America will have computers, which will be used for entertainment, for education, for the retrieval of facts, and for household management. By 1984, even many animated films will be produced with the aid of computers, which will ink character outlines, paint their interiors with solid colors, and perform crude in-betweening from key frame to key frame.

These are not blue-sky predictions. They do not depend upon whether those active in the field of "artificial intelligence" succeed in the construction of intelligent robots. Rather, the statements are conservative projections from trends and conditions that exist today.

There is significant disagreement about whether some of these changes are for good or for evil. There is significant disagreement about the pace of change that we should expect. There is some disagreement about whether this change can be controlled, although most people feel that it cannot be controlled. However, there is little disagreement with the statement that most people are fearful of these changes, that they feel intimidated by computer technology, that they feel they do not understand computers, and, even worse, that they *cannot* understand computers.

This is a pity, because as Theodor Nelson puts it so well, "Any nitwit can understand computers; and many do." Nelson has coined the term "cybercrud" to denote "putting things over on people using computers." Some of the most insidious fiction perpetrated by the computer priesthood of the 1960s and 1970s was that computers are mysterious and that only mathematical geniuses can understand them. And these notions have been swallowed hook, line, and sinker by a public mistrustful of this new technology, alientated by other technologies, and generally too accustomed to abrogating their judgment to specialists.

Dominic Covvey and Neil McAlister have produced for a lay audience a document that presents and explains clearly many of the fundamentals of modern computer technology. It is written in plain English, in a style that is forceful but unassuming, technically precise but not intimidating. It is particularly valuable in that it presents a far more comprehensive treatment of the computer as part of a *system* of humans and machines than do most books of its kind. It is written with a sensitivity for the nonspecialist that is characteristic of their professional work, which has been spent in applying computers to cardiovascular research, in relating advances in computer technology to problems in medicine, and in interpreting these advances to those in the medical profession. In writing this book, Dominic and Neil have struck their own blow in behalf of computer literacy for all and against the further spread of cybercrud. We are grateful to them for doing so.

Ronald Baecker

Associate Professor of Computer Science
Associate Professor of Electrical Engineering
University of Toronto
President
Human Computing Resources Corporation

Contents

SOFTWARE   113

PART

PRELIMINARIES

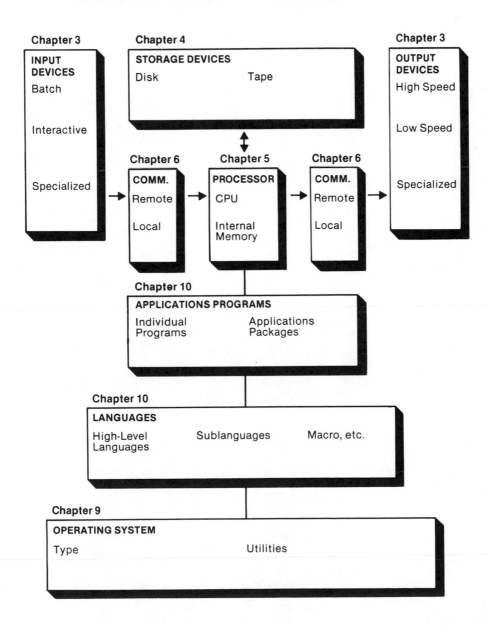

Chapter 3

INPUT DEVICES

Batch

Interactive

Specialized

Chapter 4

STORAGE DEVICES

Disk   Tape

Chapter 3

OUTPUT DEVICES

High Speed

Low Speed

Specialized

Chapter 6

COMM.

Remote

Local

Chapter 5

PROCESSOR

CPU

Internal Memory

Chapter 6

COMM.

Remote

Local

Chapter 10

APPLICATIONS PROGRAMS

Individual Programs   Applications Packages

Chapter 10

LANGUAGES

High-Level Languages   Sublanguages   Macro, etc.

Chapter 9

OPERATING SYSTEM

Type   Utilities

1

Introduction

Keeping Up With the Babbages

Computers have become an all-pervasive influence in everyday life. Whenever you do business with a bank, use a credit card, make an airline reservation, or place a long-distance telephone call, there is a good chance that a computer is involved somewhere in the transaction. Should illness strike you, your doctor may use a computer to help diagnose your illness, monitor your vital signs, and perhaps in the near future, treat you as well.

Inexpensive microcomputer systems are being aggressively marketed, and eagerly purchased, for everything — from accounting in small businesses to inventory control in the corner grocery. On a personal level, large numbers of hobby computer enthusiasts are buying their own microcomputer systems; often they program these machines themselves. Most scientists, mathematicians, and engineers own at least one programmable calculator.

The computer revolution is old news, and as with other profound changes that have affected modern life, there was no official starting gun; the revolution overtook us while we were busy doing other things.

A decade ago, a computer in the office was something to talk about. Today, such equipment is commonplace. University students routinely use computers as tools to assist their work in other fields. Our children will soon be studying computer programming in school — if they are not doing so already.

Is there any question about whether computers will play a part in your life? For better or for worse; for richer, for poorer; in sickness and in health, computers are here to stay. The choice facing us is simple: Will we let automation affect us, or will we affect automation? Those who learn how to cope with computers will be able to avoid many of the drawbacks, and enjoy more of the benefits.

In the 1980s, understanding computers is no longer a mere problem of prestige, or keeping up with the Babbages, or even keeping up with your children. Survival on the job, survival in the classroom, and survival in society depends on it.

Relatively few of the people who will be called upon to make decisions about computer systems — even big, expensive decisions — will have the time or interest to do advanced study in this field. Those decision makers will call upon computer specialists to implement their decisions. Just as you the user don't totally understand the computer, these specialists cannot be expected to understand your business, institution, or personal interests as well as you do. Therefore, the first step in coming to grips with automation is communication: communication between user and implementor.

But where do you begin? Although libraries are full of computer science textbooks and professional journals, most of this literature is written for computer scientists — or at least for people who want to know how to program. What about the person who simply needs a reasonable overview of a very complicated subject; who has no ambition to become a computer technologist? What about the person who hasn't the time to sift through thousands of books and articles to glean the relatively few pieces of information that are relevant to a nontechnical computer user?

WHAT THIS BOOK IS

This book is an attempt to compile — in one volume— a large amount of general introductory material from widely dispersed sources. The goal is to provide a simple but adequate introduction to computer machinery and programming concepts to people who have no previous knowledge of the subject. Explanations are given at the "overview" level suitable for noncomputer scientists, as opposed to the level of technical detail that would be appropriate for student computer scientists or electrical engineers. There are no circuit diagrams in this book — just functional explanations of how the "black box" works, from the user's point of view. This book is conceived as an aid to help people acquire sufficient background to think about computers on a general level. This information should enable those who become involved in computing projects to ask the proper questions of systems developers and to observe and monitor the progress of their computing projects, while figuratively looking over the shoulders of those who are supposedly working on their behalf.

You will be led into a working knowledge of computer jargon. Key words are printed in bold face, and at the end of each chapter all such key words are listed. There is a glossary at the end of the book that defines all key words.

Throughout, an effort has been made to present the wide variety of modern computing hardware and software as a spectrum of alternatives from which appropriate selections can be made for different computing applications.

A TWO-EDGED SWORD

It is reasonable to want to keep up with the leading edge of technology, but one must realize that the edge is sharp and can cut both ways. While computer science has made possible many important improvements in the human condition, there can still be significant problems even when things go relatively well for a computer application. In industry, for example, the computer has drastically changed the way we do business. This transformation has had some positive effects, but it has also been accompanied by maddening difficulties: incorrect billings, late shipments, cancelled subscriptions.

Now that computers have become an inevitable and increasingly-prevalent part of our lives, ever more viligance is required to ensure that mistakes are not perpetuated and multiplied.

To do this, we must separate computer fact from computer fantasy. The first step in coping with computers is to recognize them for what they are and to dispel unwarranted fears.

THE REAL COMPUTER

If we view the computer as capable of intelligent — or "people-like" — thought, then when something goes wrong conveniently we blame "computer error." If we see the computer as a conceptual cornucopia containing all possible solutions to all possible problems, then we will use it indiscriminately and with a high rate of failure. If we think of the computer as the ultimate vehicle to transport us into the future, then we may blindly climb aboard this technology as an agent of "progress" without knowing precisely where we want it to take us. If we feel that the computer represents the pot of gold at the end of the scientific rainbow, then its existence will soon become an end in itself, and the focus of work that requires assistance from automation will shift insidiously from the original topics of investigation to research on the computer system itself. If we covet the computer as a modern philosopher's stone capable of transmuting base data into valuable information without human thought, then we will waste our time on fruitless electronic alchemy. If the computer is in our minds a conspicuous status symbol of the scientific and business communities, then we will spend a lot of money on meaningless trinkets. If we view the computer as the ultimate toy, then in childish glee we will play with this technology, frittering away time and energy on "gee-whiz" applications of no real significance. But, we should consider the computer as a tool — a very powerful tool — but a tool.

The computer *is* an agent of change. Its uncontrolled application may metamorphose our institutions — not in beneficial ways that correct existing problems, but in ways that we do not intend. If we ignore its potential to become a giant freezer that can solidify procedures and perceptions, then general obsolescence may imperceptably overtake those functions to which we apply automation. If we fail to see a computer system as a queen ant that surrounds itself with an entire staff of workers, then we will fail to make adequate preparation for the inclusion of these workers in our working environments, with the result that our systems will not be able to fulfill their potentials. If we fail to appreciate that the computer can be a greedy cookie monster, then we may be unpleasantly surprised to find more and more of our economic resources disappearing down its hungry throat. Finally, if we fail to fear the computer's ability to become a latter-day Baal who demands our sacrifices upon the altar of technology, then we may, unresistingly, become first its worshipers, and finally its sacrifices.

The danger with automation is not the computer itself: it is how we perceive and use the computer.

COMPUTER CONCIOUSNESS

Those who appreciate computers as machines realize that a bureaucratic foul-up is a human error. People who understand the magic buzzwords of computer science are unlikely to be impressed or cowed by them. Well-informed customers will ignore sales-pitches appealing to their egos: marketers will be forced to concentrate on the real issues, like cost and benefit.

The user, who has a realistic idea of what computers can do, can avoid wasting energy and money on trivial, superfluous applications, can shun the temptation to invoke the magic of "computerization" in the quest of impossible glories, and can appreciate those uses of computers that can be truly beneficial.

The 80s have arrived. The future is now. Coping with computers is a fact of life: coping successfully is a matter of survival!

NOTES

1. Wilkes, M. V., In *Encyclopedia of Computer Science,* edited by A. Ralston and C. L. Meek, New York: Petrocelli/Charter, 1976, p. 157.
2. J. Weizenbaum, *Computer Power and Human Reason.* San Francisco, W. H. Freeman Co., 1976.

2

Computer Systems

OBJECTIVES

Prerequisite to the effective use of computers to solve problems in any environment is the establishment of appropriate **computer systems** in that environment. The use of the word "system" is important, for it implies a rational mixture of integrated parts working synergistically to form a useful whole. In order to gain a basic understanding of the "gross anatomy" of computer systems, it is helpful to separate these systems, somewhat artificially, into components. This is what we will attempt to do in this section.

What are the parts that make up a computer system? Broadly speaking, such systems are composed of two parts.

The first part is **hardware** — the physical, electronic, and electromechanical devices that we instantly recognize and think of as "computers." the second part is **software** — the programs that control and coordinate the activities of the computer hardware and that direct the processing of data.

The success or failure of any computer system depends on the skill with which these components are selected and blended. Too frequently, critical decisions regarding the selection and acquisition of components of the computer system are determined either by random chance or by the persuasion of computer sales personnel. Some users are lucky and do obtain useful systems in this manner, but inevitably many others are not so lucky. A poorly chosen system can be a monstrosity incapable of performing the tasks for which it was originally acquired.

The danger of an ungainly system that cannot meet its goals is not only failure but also poorly utilized finances. A bad system may be a technical and economic albatross hanging around the neck of the department or institution responsible for it.

In the discussion of hardware components and types of software, a rather loose metaphor of "evolution" is followed. The development of the various components of a computer system has been in some ways a story of "survival of the fittest." At any particular time, the "fittest" component is the one that provides best performance at the lowest cost. Over the decades that computers have been in existence, advancing technology and automation theory have rendered obsolete some devices or concepts that were serviceable in their day. On the other hand, machines and theories that have been able to respond to "evolutionary pressures" have proliferated and given rise to numerous more sophisticated descendents.

Whether evolving computer science theory (which often precedes reality by many years) has actually provided the impetus for new developments in hardware and software, or whether computer scientists have mainly figured out what to do with technology *after* it has been made available is a matter of debate — perhaps never to be resolved. One can only observe that the technological imperative often seems to lead to remarkable technical developments in the absence of any justifiable need. Undeniably, computers are subject to possible abuse: They can make possible a delivery system for nuclear weapons. On the other hand, in the medical and health-care fields, computers can potentially provide one of the most productive uses of technology for the betterment of humankind.

The "evolutionary pressures" at work today seem to be concerned mainly with money. Therefore, in the long run the role of computers in society may be dictated by the degree to which they can demonstrably reduce costs. So far they have not always been successful in this regard. However, evolution is at work, and only time will yield the final verdict.

The computer user must know some computer system theory and also where and how these systems can be obtained. Therefore we shall give some attention to the practical considerations of selecting, pricing, and obtaining hardware and software. We may be entering a fairly stable period in total computer system cost. Although the cost of hardware has been declining in the past several years, labor costs — and consequently, the cost of software development — have been increasing at the same time. Therefore, the total cost of the complete computer system (both hardware and software) has leveled out and probably will not decline much further (Fig. 2.1).

A computer system does not exist in a vacuum. It is always a part of a larger human "system" — less easily defined, but no less real than the computer hardware and software components. For instance, some computer systems serve as part of an instrument, such as in a CT scanner. To be useful, such computers are carefully interfaced with the instrument, appropriately programmed, and expected to work in synergy with the other parts of the instrument. Other computers are integrated into departments or institutions such as hospitals. These computers must function in this large milieu in ways analogous to how they function in an instrument. In the largest applications, a computer system may be only one component of a very large regional project. In short, a computer system should never be an end in itself. Its success or failure is measured by the success it effects in the situation in which it is used.

Therefore, if computer systems are to serve people's needs they must be carefully integrated into the human and procedural domain they are intended to improve. The computer system cannot do all the adapting, though. The human milieu must also be groomed to accept the computer system. People's fears, concerns, and even foolish prejudices must be faced and rationalized. A delicate balance will be struck between the human engineering of computer systems and the educating of potential users to make realistic, attainable demands on such systems.

THE COMPUTER CONFIGURATION

Hardware

Figure 2.2 shows schematically the fundamental components of computer hardware joined together in a computer system. The centerpiece is variously called the **computer,** the **processor,** or usually the **central processing unit** (**CPU**). We use the term "computer" loosely to include those parts of the hardware in which calculations and other data manipulations are performed, and the high-speed in-

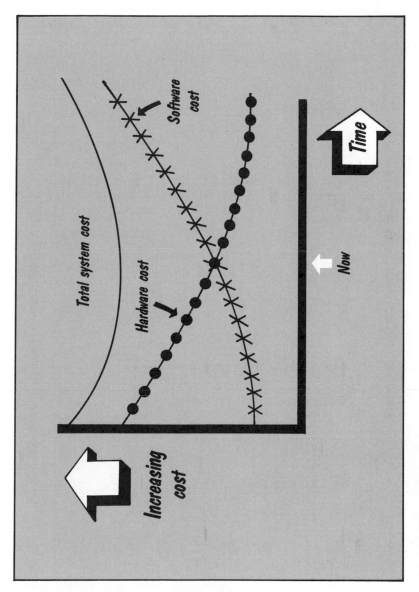

Fig. 2.1. The costs of computer systems in recent years

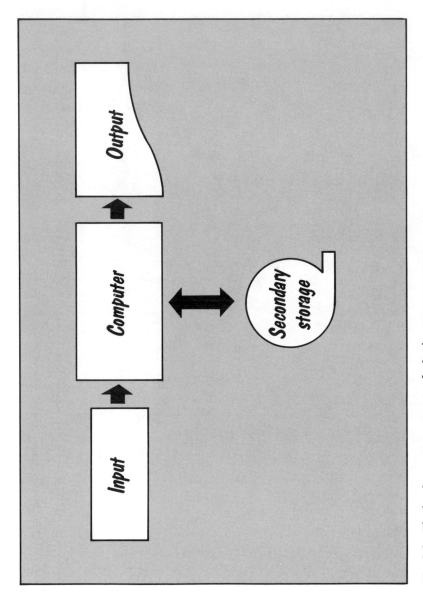

Fig. 2.2. The hardware components of a basic computer system

ternal memory in which data and instructions are stored during actual execution of programs. These two components (cf. **computer system**) are normally housed in the same enclosure; it makes sense to think of them together. Attached to the CPU are the various **peripheral devices**. **Input devices** are used to enter data or programs into the computer for processing; punched card readers and keyboards are two common examples of input devices. After processing data, the computer gives its answers back to us through **output devices**; printers and video screens are two examples. When data or programs must be saved for long periods of time, they are stored on various **secondary memory devices** (or **storage devices**) — magnetic tape or magnetic disk, for instance.

Peripheral devices are usually electromechanical in nature, and as such their rate of performance is many orders of magnitude slower than the purely electronic circuits of the computer itself. For this reason, input, output, and storage operations are often the rate-limiting operations in computer processing of data. The CPU is often idle, waiting for the electromechanical peripheral devices to catch up with it. Since the CPU often has the potential to work much faster than any one task demands of it, in some kinds of systems this feature is exploited so that many users can employ the same computer without mutual interference.

Software

Computer software can be divided into two very broad categories — systems software, and applications software. Applications software is often simply referred to as **programs**.

Systems software is further divided into two general types: operating systems and programming languages. **Operating systems** are the master programs that coordinate the activities of all hardware and software resources in a computer system. In a multi-user environment, operating systems also coordinate the activities of all system users, so that they do not interfere with each other while sharing the system. Normally, computer programmers write their applications programs conveniently in a human-readable **programming language**. Programs written in a programming language must be translated from human-understandable statements to the machine instructions that the computer system can perform. The systems software that does this, depending on its design, is called a **compiler,** or an **interpreter.**

Applications programs, when brought into internal memory, direct the computer to perform particular tasks for users. They may be provided along with the hardware by a systems supplier as part of a computer product designed to answer a specific need in some areas. These complete hardware/software products are called **turnkey systems. Software packages** (groups of applications programs) for general application categories such as statistics may be purchased, leased, or rented by users, who select the packages that most closely correspond to their individual needs. For many applications unique programs are written, either by an outside developer or by the user's own in-house computer group.

With this brief orientation we may now look more closely at the constituent parts of computer systems. In the following chapters, we shall deal in far greater detail with the topics mentioned only briefly here.

NEW WORDS

applications program	peripheral device
central processing unit (CPU)	processor
compiler	program
computer	programming language
computer system	secondary memory device
hardware	software
input device	software package
interpreter	storage device
operating system	turnkey system
output device	

PART

HARDWARE

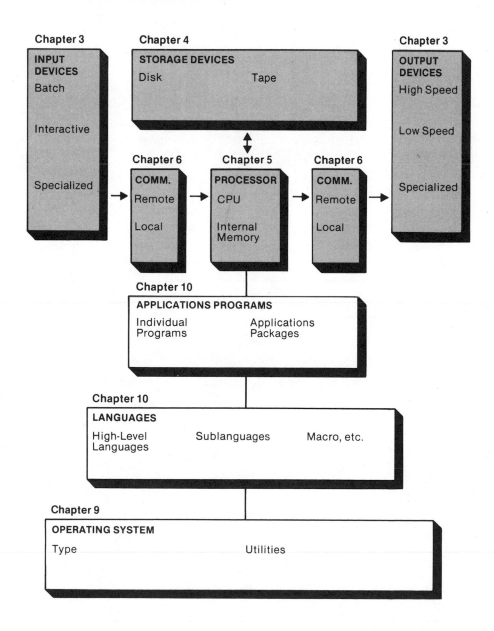

Chapter 3

INPUT
DEVICES

Batch

Interactive

Specialized

Chapter 4

STORAGE DEVICES

Disk   Tape

Chapter 3

OUTPUT
DEVICES

High Speed

Low Speed

Specialized

Chapter 6

COMM.

Remote

Local

Chapter 5

PROCESSOR

CPU

Internal
Memory

Chapter 6

COMM.

Remote

Local

Chapter 10

APPLICATIONS PROGRAMS

Individual   Applications
Programs   Packages

Chapter 10

LANGUAGES

High-Level   Sublanguages   Macro, etc.
Languages

Chapter 9

OPERATING SYSTEM

Type   Utilities

3

Fauna of the Solid-State Stone Age

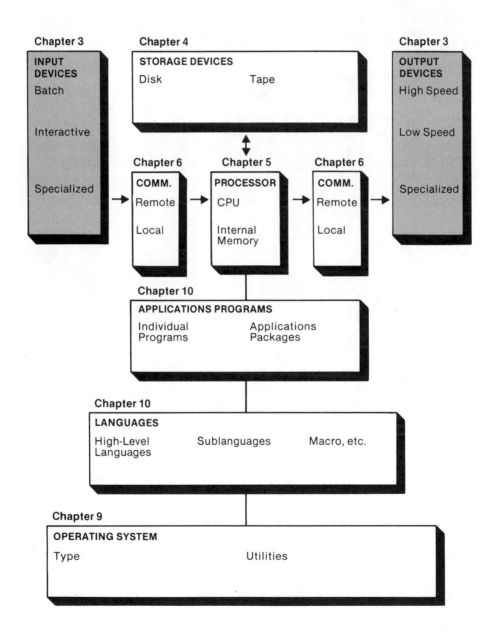

Input Devices

It is appropriate to begin the study of computer hardware by examining those machines that are used to enter information into a computer, namely, input devices. However, even this seemingly straightforward step is not as simple as one might hope.

THE DESCENT OF LANGUAGE IN THE COMPUTER AGE

In primeval times humans began to organize their grunts and cries into a convenient means of communication — formal language. Elegant, descriptive language may have reached a peak somewhere between the works of Homer and Kipling, but we, the subjects of mass media input, might be convinced that language has passed its zenith and is now regressing back to primitive grunts and cries. Certainly, the routine vocabulary of pop singers and television sports announcers tends to support this contention.

The quality of the spoken and written word may not really be declining in the twentieth century, but the advent of human–computer communication has forced us to communicate unnaturally with switches, punched cards, and other such media that we all find frustrating and confusing. The general trend of this evolutionary process is shown in Fig. 3.1.

EVOLUTION OF INPUT DEVICES

Today a menagerie of devices is available for communication with computers. These are summarized in the phylogeny of Fig. 3.2. All can be classified as some form of input device. Although none of these input devices allow the operator to converse in everyday human speech, an evolutionary trend is discernible. Each improvement is a step closer toward natural language on a continuum from human to machine (Fig. 3.3). Each step closer does imply higher costs, but usually the reward is more sophisticated devices that require less and less human adaptation.

Let us examine the various orders of devices in the input kingdom. Each of its members has specific advantages and disadvantages, and knowledge of these is essential when designing or evaluating systems for use in any particular application.

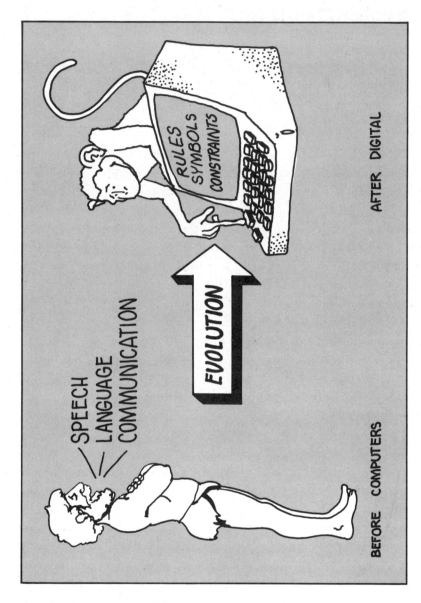

Fig. 3.1. Evolution of language in the Computer Age
In talking to a computer, one is constrained by the severe limitations of the machine's ability to understand — a great step backward in communication!

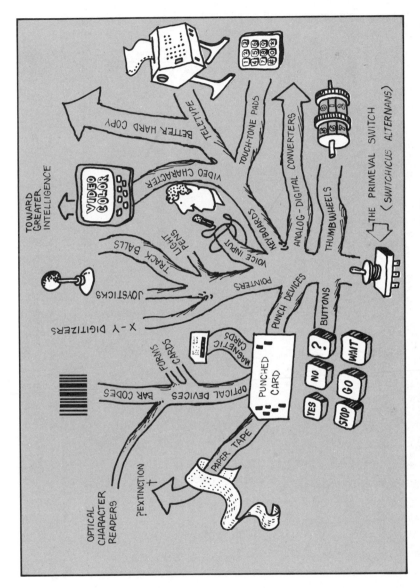

Fig. 3.2. Evolution of the Input Kingdom
Our own simplified phylogeny of input devices.

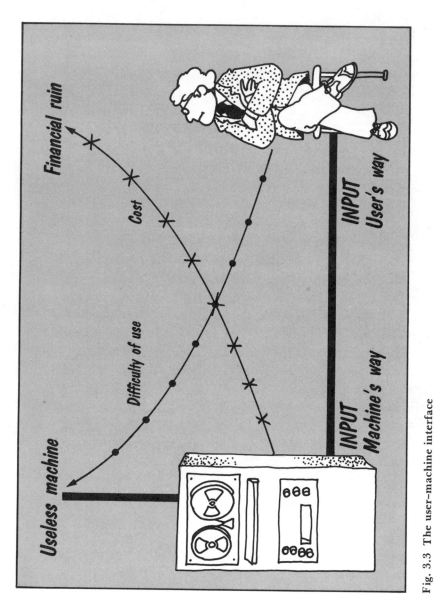

Fig. 3.3 The user-machine interface

People and computers must reach a compromise in order to communicate. The more sophisticated the input device, the less effort is required to adapt to it. The goal is to come as close to the user's way of doing things as you can afford and as current technology permits.

THE SWITCH FAMILY

At the bottom of the evolutionary heap is the lowly switch. Users "talking" to computers at this level must have intimate knowledge of numerical machine language, since each switch represents either 1 (one) or 0 (zero) — the form in which data is stored in computer memory. Because the switch is so fundamental and inexpensive, it has survived from the times of early computer history (35 years ago) into the present era, where it still proliferates on the front panels of hobby microcomputers. Switches, however, have no place in modern input systems except to indicate simple events.

First cousins to the switch are two devices — panels of buttons, and "thumbwheels" or dials. These devices are simple but they can have a useful place in computer products designed for specific applications. At times it is easier to push a button to start a process or to use a thumbwheel to enter a value than to type the information on a keyboard. A convenient and useful variant of push-button panels is an ordinary touch-tone telephone, with its pad of 12 buttons. After punching in the phone number of a computer in the usual way, one can use the touch-tone pad as an input device. If desired, a mask can be placed over the buttons to associate each button with a specific function. With such a device, even a person with little technical knowledge can easily input information into the computer. In the United States such a system has been used on an experimental basis to enter medical billing information into remote computers. Computer-generated voice is used to verify input and to produce output (usually numeric). Thus, when you rent a touch-tone telephone, the telephone company also gives you an input device at no extra charge!

PUNCHED CARDS AND RELATED SPECIES

The concept of using cards with holes to provide input to a machine is very old. A weaving machine of the Industrial Revolution used punched cards to direct its operation. Perhaps the most familiar modern descendent of this antique device is the ubiquitous **punched card**, still favored by many companies for billing. The punched card still provides a cheap, easy means of input to batch-processing computers. Cards hold up to 80 **characters** of information (a character is a letter, number, or punctuation mark). The input speed of punched cards is usually over 400 characters/second (300 cards/minute). For comparison, the average input speed of a typist is much slower — roughly one character/second. Because of this difference, one card reader can serve as an input device for many clerks producing punched cards.

Normally, a special device called a **keypunch** is required to make punched cards. The keypunch types what the pattern of punched holes means along the top edge of the card so that a person can read it. There are also cards that can be perforated with a stylus. Although this process is slower, it does not require fancy equipment and is not as noisy as the keypunch. Thus these stylus-perforated cards can be prepared without disturbing other people in an office. They can be useful for the preparation of small amounts of input on a casual basis, without the need of investing in a keypunch. A fairly inexpensive mechanical device that punches one character at a time is also available for people who must prepare small amounts of card input.

An early relative of the punched card is continuous **paper tape**. Once made, a paper tape cannot easily be modified or read by people, so it is a less useful medium than cards. Therefore, this species may soon be extinct.

After punched cards had been around for many years, someone had an inspiration: Why not do away with the perforations and make a pencil mark instead of a hole? This input medium is called the **optical mark card**. In all respects the card looks similar to a punched card, except for the absence of the holes. A device for reading these cards called an **optical mark recognition reader (OMR reader)** can cost as little as $1000.

A logical extension of the optical mark card is the **optical mark form**, a piece of paper 8½ × 11 inches, on which both descriptive material and multiple-choice selections can be printed. Answers can be indicated in little boxes by marking with a pencil. These forms can then be input to a computer via a reader that costs from $3000 to well over $20,000, depending on the degree of sophistication. Optical mark forms have been used to record and process psychological test data.

Both of these optical mark media depend on special forms (full-page forms cost 10–50¢ per page); each form has carefully aligned columns reserved for pencil marks. A dramatic adaptation beyond these confines is **optical character recognition (OCR)**, or optically readable characters. These special computer-readable fonts got off to an early start when **magnetic-ink computer-readable (MICR)** numerals were invented for processing checks in banks. Luckily, devices that recognize characters optically, as opposed to magnetically, can be built. The optically readable fonts (OCR-A and OCR-B) can be printed with ordinary typewriters using a carbon ribbon. A Selectric typeball is available with these fonts. A machine that reads OCR input into a computer is expensive, typically costing at least $15,000–$25,000. The advantage here is that the input device is a typewriter: The office typewriter takes the place of the key-punch machine, and the input is readable both by machine and by person with equal ease.

A peculiar variant in the OCR world is a typewriter "golf ball" that makes tiny bar codes below each character. We read the regular typing; a special bar code reader can decipher the bar codes. The primary advantage here is that the bar code reader is much cheaper. Another device exists that is held in the hand and manually scans over lines of OCR-A type. This device costs less than $10,000.

Some work has been done to develop input devices that recognize any font and any size of print, so that any typewritten input (or at least a large variety of fonts) can be fed directly into a computer. So far, such machines are usually out of the price range of all but the largest operations and are therefore impractial in most clerical applications.

There are systems in operation that use a defined style of hand-printed numerics; one such system is used in one hospital to read psychiatric out-patient registration data and hand-printed numeric data concerning ambulance calls. Finally, some people are experimenting with machines that interpret ordinary handwriting as input, but this type of device is still only experimental.

A remotely related derivative of cards is the **magnetic strip card** that resembles an ordinary credit card. Until quite recently such cards were expensive and could hold little information. However, work is under way to pack much more information onto these cards (some now hold 1000 characters), and to lower the price. A conceivable medical application for such an input medium might be an ambulatory medical record that a patient could carry like a credit card. Systems have been in existence for a number of years to record analog (continuous) information on magnetic strips on ordinary keypunch cards.

KEYBOARD VARIATIONS

The keyboard is usually the most available device for input to a computer. Keyboards have evolved from the clumsy and noisy **teletype** keyboard into easy-to-use devices that are part of video terminals that electronically display input as it is being entered. Teletype-like devices provide **hard copy** on paper, whereas video terminals (or **CRT terminals**) do not. When there is no need for a permanent record of input, and high-speed output is desired, a video terminal is preferable.

Hard-copy terminals are generally one of two types: impact or nonimpact. In impact terminals, noise is a factor too seldom considered. Many impact terminals are extremely noisy and may be intolerable in an office; nonimpact terminals are quiet. A hard-copy terminal typically costs $1500–$4000.

Basic models of video terminals carry price tages of $1500–$2000 but the price is expected to fall to $1000 or less in the near future. Another advantage of video terminals is that they are more reliable than hard-copy terminals. Hobby versions cost under $500.

When considering an input terminal, one must do some rather hard thinking about the application. Some terminals transmit one character at a time, as typed on the keyboard. These are referred to as **dumb terminals,** and they are the cheapest kind. However, other terminals are available for use with computer systems that are programmed to accept information in blocks (or groups) of characters. These terminals allow data preparation under the control of the terminal alone; the terminal is then able to transmit this preprepared data to a remote computer system. It may be advantageous under some circumstances to employ these **smart terminals,** which can save up many characters and then send them when the user and computer are ready. This can significantly reduce communication costs when the computer is remote, and also reduce the load on the computer since the terminal itself handles data acquisition. Indeed, some terminals are so smart (the term **intelligent terminals** has been coined to describe them) that they can be used to correct and edit text or to perform computations or checks on data before it is sent to the central computer. Smart terminals are considerably more expensive than their dumb relatives, but units with prices in the $4000–$6000 range are now available, and these will have important implications in data acquisition, especially related to databases.

EXOTIC CREATURES: THE NEWEST INPUT DEVICES

An offshoot of the optical mark family, **bar code** schemes, can be found on anything from cereal boxes to railroad cars. The advantages of bar codes are that they can be applied to any surface and that they can be read by a simple and inexpensive device called a **wand.** A bar code label printer costs about $6000, but the wand that reads bar codes as computer input costs less than $1000 and is becoming cheaper. In medicine, bar codes have found a home in some radiology departments, where they are used to identify X-ray films and to help keep track of their location. We have already mentioned the hybrid species between OCR and bar codes.

A whole new genus of input devices has arisen in conjunction with video displays. A **light pen** can be pointed at a screen for the selection of one of a list of choices presented to an operator, or for inputting drawings. Some displays go one step further: They can sense a finger pointed at the data on the screen. This sounds quite exotic, but in fact one can convert a regular display screen to a touch-input device with about four hundred dollars of add-on equipment.

There are still other strange input devices available for special applications. **X-Y digitizers** track a stylus or a pointer in two-dimensional space by one of a variety of electronic and mechanical methods. These digitizers find practical applications, for instance, in the entry of drawings and building plans into systems to assist in architectural design. **Track balls** or **joysticks** can also be used for drawing continuous lines or for pointing. Joysticks can be found in many popular computer-video games.

Of particular interest in signal-processing applications are the so-called **analog-to-digital converters** that transform continuous electronic signals into the digital (quantized) information that a computer can process. Such devices take an electrical waveform — unacceptable as input to a computer — and change it into a sequence of discrete numbers that a computer can accept.

FUTURE MUTATIONS

Highest on the evolutionary ladder of input devices would be those that understand everyday human language — typed, handwritten, and ultimately spoken.

At present, however, natural-language processing in any form is only a dream. There are some input devices that interpret voice commands — usually a very limited number of words. They have been used experimentally in an automatic airline reservation system and in supermarkets for tallying prices. But these voice input systems are still experimental, limited, and expensive. The use of voice input must be carefully limited to the problem at hand; there is as yet no computer capable of comprehending ordinary spoken language, and the introduction of such a device is not probable in the immediate future.

Computers cannot understand people on people's terms. Because humans are more flexible, we continue to hold the responsibility to mold our thinking and ways of communicating to the computer's admittedly odd specifications.

THE USER–MACHINE INTERFACE

We have briefly reviewed the different classes of input devices that abound today. There are many levels of sophistication and expense. Several fundamentals will be appreciated: Sophistication costs money; the most sophisticated device may not be the one that you need; some features that *are* required in a given application are easy to overlook until deficiencies become self-evident. Hunting for the appropriate input device is important in establishing or evaluating any computer system that must get input from people. Armed with this information, you will at least know what beasts to look for.

Output Devices

We have discussed the various phyla of devices used by people to input information into computers. Now let us consider the converse: the means by which computers output their answers to people. Today, although computers cannot understand input in human terms, evolution in the Output Kingdom has proceeded from humble beginnings to the point where there are now many kinds of output devices that communicate with us in everyday, perfectly understandable ways. (See Fig. 3.4.)

LET THERE BE LIGHT!

In the beginning, the first output device to emerge from the gloom was the simple **sense light**. When the light was on, it indicated some arbitrary condition. Members of this species tend to nest together as arrays of lights, still used to signify the storage of a 1 (one, meaning "on") or a 0 (zero, meaning "off") in individual computer memory cells (**bits**). These arrays display the numeric contents of various registers or of **locations** in memory (a location is a group of cells or bits) in **binary** format (the number system based on powers of two instead of the powers of ten used in our decimal system). Binary output is simple and inexpensive, and consequently lights are the only output devices on some of the cheapest hobby microcomputers. Because it is also the most direct means of getting at a com-

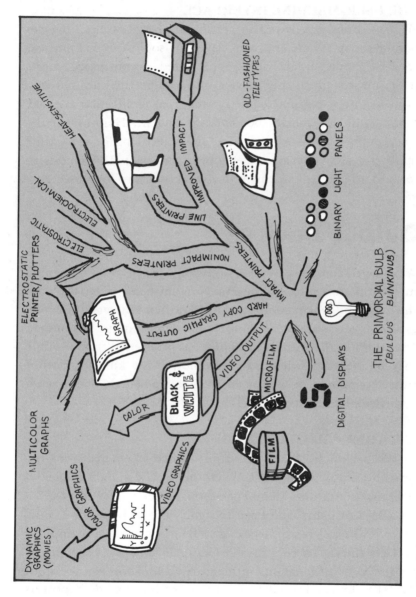

Fig. 3.4. The Output Kingdom
This schematic tree illustrates the principal orders of output devices. More recent devices are situated around the periphery of the tree.

puter's innards, a binary light panel is found on most commercial computers, where it is used by repair personnel for "debugging" (figuring out and correcting) hardware problems. Light panels, used to display decimal values, are still used heavily in instrumentation and are now familiar to millions in the form of light-emitting diode or liquid-crystal displays on watches and calculators. Some radio-activity counting devices use such output.

THE PRINTER FAMILY: THE GOOD, THE BAD, AND THE UGLY

The average user, however, cannot translate binary light patterns into useful information. Early in the evolution of computers it became obvious that more appropriate, human-readable output media were essential. Therefore, computer-driven typewriters appeared on the scene quite early in the developmental timetable. These first devices were similar to the still familiar teletype: They were slow and noisy, but they did give printed (**hard copy**) output that people could understand and carry away with them. Impact-printing terminals still thrive, but over the eons — about 35 years — some subspecies have emerged, each of which provides unique features. Certain modern printers, for instance, give letter-quality — i.e., suitable for correspondence — type in selectable typefaces, even on regular letterhead paper attached to a continuous roll of carrier paper. From 10 to 45 characters per second (CPS) is the typical speed range for impact printers. Any application that requires the production of printed reports will need hard-copy printers.

To simplify the mechanical apparatus, to increase printing speed, and to make printed output quieter, a different order of printers has evolved. This type of printer attempts to produce similar results through a different anatomical arrangement. **Dot matrix** characters are created by printing dots on the paper in an array, typically 5 X 7 for capital letters only or 7 X 9 for upper- and lower-case characters. The dots are printed by a column of little wires on a head that moves horizontally to scan out each dot matrix character on a line. The more dense the matrix, the better the quality of the output.

However, it is obvious that the broken style of dot matrix is never as legible or as elegant as "typewriter" (solid type) printing.

Noisy output devices such as impact printers are troublesome and there have been many attempts to quiet them. The ultimate in the quest for silence are the nonimpact printers. Of these, the one relevant to this discussion is the dot matrix character printer that produces output on special heat-sensitive paper by burning dots onto it. Some devices of this type, typically capable of printing 30 CPS, are suitable for use in the quietest office. Another type of nonimpact printer is the higher-speed magnetic printer that can produce output not simply on paper, but on any surface, as was recently illustrated in a magazine ad in which a sales blurb noted that output on cloth underwear could even be produced! Finally, an inexpensive, though low-quality output device is becoming popular for instrumentation applications. This particular device is called an electroconductive paper printer and sells for as little as $300.

These hard-copy output devices that print one character at a time are relatively inexpensive — typically under $2000 and up to $3000–$5000 for letter-quality. One disadvantage is low speed. When there is a large amount of output to be printed, higher speed is mandatory. To fill this ecological niche there arose the **line printer**, a printing device that prints about as many *lines* per second as slower printers print *characters* per second. There are many impact line printers. A typical device uses a revolving belt containing multiple complete alphabetic and numeric character sets. At any given moment, several characters of a line to be printed may be positioned correctly in a row across a page, and therefore the belt can be struck simultaneously by multiple hammers in order to print several characters on the line at once. These machines achieve very high-speed output — typically 300 lines per minute (LPM) of 132 columns, which is $(132 \times 300)/60 = 660$ CPS maximum. A realistic price range for a line printer of this speed is $10,000–$15,000; however, high-speed dot matrix variants (also sometimes called line printers) are usually less expensive. Although the typeface is solid, line printers usually produce the lowest quality of printed output. It is sometimes difficult to distinguish O's (ohs) from 0's (zeros) and often characters on the same line are not well aligned. Another significant drawback is that line printers are so noisy that their operation can usually not be tolerated in a public area. Also problematic is the fact that line printers are usually connected directly to the computer (parallel interface) and therefore cannot be located remotely (serial transmission) without expensive receiving controllers (remote job terminal). Very high-speed varieties of line printers exist; however, their cost increases rapidly with their speed.

Equally swift but much less noisy than the average line printer are the nonimpact electrochemical and electrostatic printers. For $4000 one can buy a virtually silent 80-column, 2400-line-per-minute (3200 CPS) electrostatic printer that uses continuous unperforated paper or fanfold (Z-fold) perforated paper costing about 2¢ per foot. Most electrostatic printers, though, are in the 600-LPM speed and $5000–$15,000 price range. The printing process used here is similar to that employed in Xerox copiers.

Figure 3.5 sets forth the functional characteristics by which hard-copy printers should be evaluated for use in particular applications.

PUNCHED OUTPUT

Some of the more ancient families of output devices produce computer-generated punched cards or punched paper tape. These media are not human-readable. Punched cards can be **interpreted,** a process that prints the characters encoded by the holes across the top of each card. However, no such process exists for paper tape. Punched output retains usefulness when a cheap machine-readable storage medium is required for data that is examined or analyzed only rarely.

COMPUTER OUTPUT MICROFILM

A high-speed, high-density output medium particularly useful for archival functions is microfilm, produced directly by computer **(computer output microfilm** or COM). COM production can be done either on site or at a service bureau. Since COM devices are expensive,

	Reliability	Noise	Speed*	Print quality	Print color (red + black)	Multipart forms	Forms handling†			
							Friction feed	Pin feed + preprinted forms handling	Requires special paper/ toner/ etc.	Paper width continuously variable up to platen size
Impact	↓	↑	→	←	Y	Y	Y	Y	N	Y
Nonimpact	↑	↓	←	→	N	N	Y	N	Y	N

*Low- and high-speed units of each type exist but the usual case is shown.
†Each printer must be evaluated relative to its handling of continuous, pin-fed, fanfold, etc. paper.

Fig. 3.5. General characteristics of hard copy

the latter approach is often used. Data to be microfilmed can be loaded onto a magnetic tape, and this tape can then be taken to a service bureau where another machine generates microfilm output.

LIGHTS MAKE A COMEBACK

It might have seemed that light output devices had reached their ultimate evolutionary stage as simple indicator arrays. Not so. They have evolved into our most flexible output devices!

For many interactions with computers a permanent record is unnecessary. Output that is scanned once and then discarded generates a lot of wasted paper. To solve this problem, **cathode ray tube (CRT) terminals** arose. Not only do these terminals eliminate paper waste, but they also are completely silent and frequently much faster than hard-copy terminals. Their remarkable ability to fill a screen almost instantaneously with a whole "page" of information is a great asset in viewing textual records, since people tend to become frustrated while waiting for a terminal to type out text at only 30 characters per second. CRT terminals, because of their speed and quietness, are very useful interactive devices for use in offices and in other areas where speed and quietness is needed. The electronic circuitry used in them is very similar to that in the familiar TV (video) set.

The video species are diverse, agile, and colorful. The original video output was single-color ("black and white") upper-case letters. Proof that this species was no accidental mutation is the fact that simple output monitors like these are still encountered in abundance, at prices of about $1500. Microcomputer hobbyists can get even simpler versions for a few hundred dollars. In more highly developed devices, lower-case letters can be displayed, and some give options of blinking and dual-density characters. Still others can, at the user's option, produce "negative" (dark) characters on a bright background. Certain video screens can even make each character a different color if so desired — an important consideration in order to catch someone's attention when a value is abnormal. One such color terminal sells for as little as $2000.

More sophisticated screens can generate continuous lines for graphic displays. The simplest of these are monochromatic and may have strictly limited graphics applications. For example, they may use special characters strung together in order to form lines that look continuous, or they may be restricted regarding the number and shape of curves that can be drawn at once. Multicolor pictorial graphics are extremely helpful in emphasizing contrast, and have been used with good effect in nuclear medicine where differences in intensity would be too subtle if shades of only one color were used.

The full power of video output may be realized some day in the near future. Dynamic (motion) graphics output devices are presently not commercially available, but devices that output simple changing scenes have been developed for flight trainers and already work is proceeding on computer-generated movies. These devices could have important impact on the use of **computer-aided instruction (CAI)** techniques in schools.

HARD-COPY GRAPHICS

A wide variety of devices called **plotters** have met the need for permanent copy of graphic output. The first plotter used a pen that traveled back and forth across a rotating drum to which paper was attached. These devices still exist and are still doing well because they are quite accurate and reasonably fast. Other plotters feature a pen that moves in two dimensions on a flat sheet of paper; these plotters are not unlike drafting boards in appearance. Moving-pen plotters are relatively slow because they are mechanical devices and most can produce only one continuous line at a time. Complicated patterns can take a very long time to produce. On the other hand, the modern electrostatic plotter (often as an optional extension of the previously mentioned electrostatic printer) can achieve slightly less "artistic" results in seconds. This is because it does not depend on a moving pen, but rather electronically generates patterns of dots in a line across the page to make up a picture. Pen plotters have been put to great advantage in respiratory function and biochemistry labs to produce hard-copy output of simple curves.

High-speed hard-copy output may produce a blizzard of paper that people cannot handle, since computer output can be much faster than human input. Graphic output may be an effective alternative. (See Fig. 3.6). The ancient maxim that one picture is worth a thou-

Fig. 3.6. The medium is the message
A line printer can easily produce more output than people can absorb as input!
Selection of the appropriate mix of output media is crucial. Remember that the
"digestibility" of computer output is inversely proportional to its weight!

sand words still stands, particularly in instances where graphs are more useful than columns of numbers for conveying trends and giving an overview. Most of the time, a graph is not only better than columns and pages of printed numbers, but also has the advantages of being thinner, quicker to produce, and easier to file!

HYBRID SPECIES

In recent years, a whole new class of output devices has evolved to bridge the gaps between the various devices just described. For example, you can now buy a terminal with video screen *and* hard copy. Normally only the screen functions, but a paper copy of what is on the screen can be produced at the touch of a button. In this way no paper is wasted, since hard copy is produced only when a permanent record is desired. A medical application for such a device is in the area of patient registration. An admitting clerk can obtain relevant personal data from each patient, and correct and edit it on a screen. Then, only if something has changed from the previous visit, a new hard copy can be produced for the paper medical record. For approximately $5500 one can obtain a CRT terminal with a built-in electrochemical or thermal printer; many CRT terminals allow printers or other hard-copy devices to be attached to them.

There are electrostatic **printer-plotters** that produce both print and graphic displays with equal facility. These machines offer advantages over regular printers because it is possible to change the style and the size of the letters at the user's whim. In addition, they can intersperse graphs and displays among printed lines.

It is therefore evident that the previously distinct roles of printer, plotter, and graphic display are becoming blurred in modern times by cross-breeding, resulting in a few hybrid output devices capable of handling a number of roles.

UNUSUAL CREATURES

Although it is tricky to give voice input to computers, they are learning to talk with surprising ease. One reason for this fact is that it is possible to restrict the words that a computer would (literally) "say" to a small and manageable vocabulary. Appropriate words can be selected from prerecorded messages, or words can be composed from basic sounds called **phonemes**. Voice output has already been employed experimentally in an airline reservation system and in a variety of credit systems.

Another important group of devices are those whose output can be read directly by an appropriate input device. Among these are bar-code label printers, character printers whose typeface is one of the computer-readable OCR fonts, and special variants that provide both human-readable and computer-readable output.

CONCLUSION

Obtaining legible or audible output from a computer is not nearly as difficult as trying to put information into a computer. Output devices have evolved to accommodate virtually all applications and all budgets. What is important is the selection of the appropriate output medium for any given application. In the Output Kingdom (with apologies to Dr. McLuhan) the medium really is the message. But the jungle is infested with different devices having different characteristics, and before you bag one for use in your system, consider carefully whether it will obscure or enhance what your computer has to say to you.

BIBLIOGRAPHY

CRT Terminals

Anderson, H., Terminals. *Telecommunications 1977 Handbook and Buyer's Guide,* pp. 89–96.

Axner, D. H., and F. H. Reagan, Alphanumeric display terminal survey. *Datamation* 24:6:183 (June) 1978.

Stiefel, M. L., What is an "intelligent" terminal? *Mini-Micro Systems* 10:3:50 (March) 1977.

Printers

Ahrens, J., Teleprinter industry trends. *Telecommunications* 11:5:36 (May) 1977.

Axner, D. H., and F. H. Reagan, Teleprinter terminal survey. *Datamation* 24:5:232 (May) 1978.

Bowers, D. M., Printers and teleprinters. *Mini-Micro Systems* 10:1:30 (January) 1977.

Strassman, P. A., and C. F. Willard, The evolution of the page printer. *Datamation* 24:5:167 (May) 1978.

Punched Cards, Paper Tape

Bowers, D. M. et al., Punched cards and perforated paper tape equipment. *Modern Data* 8:10:65 (October) 1975.

Computer Output Microfilm

Computer output microfilm. *Modern Data* 5:12:32 (December) 1972.

Muldowney, W. J., Looking for a COM recorder? *Datamation* 24:2:143 (February) 1978.

Plotters

Orr, J. N., Computer graphics. *Mini-Micro Systems* 11:2:46 (February) 1978.

Stiefel, M. L., Digital plotter terminals and systems. *Modern Data* 4:9:47 (September) 1971.

Voice Response Systems

Voice recognition/response from perception technology. *Modern Data* 7:7:52 (November) 1974.

Voice response systems. *Modern Data* 5:11:46 (November) 1972.

Yasaki, E. K., Voice recognition comes of age. *Datamation* 22:7:65 (August) 1976.

Bar Codes

Yasaki, E. K., Bar codes for data entry. *Datamation* 21:5:63 (May) 1975.

NEW WORDS

analog-to-digital converter	hard copy
bar code	intelligent terminal
binary	interpreting
bit	joystick
cathode ray tube (CRT) terminal	keypunch
character	light pen
computer-aided instruction (CAI)	line printer
computer output microfilm (COM)	location
dot matrix	magnetic-ink computer-readable (MICR)
dumb terminal	

magnetic strip card

optical character recognition
(OCR)

optical mark card

optical mark form

optical mark recognition reader
(OMR reader)

paper tape

phoneme

plotter

printer-plotter

punched card

sense light

smart terminal

teletype

terminal

track ball

wand

X-Y digitizer

4

Never Forgetting

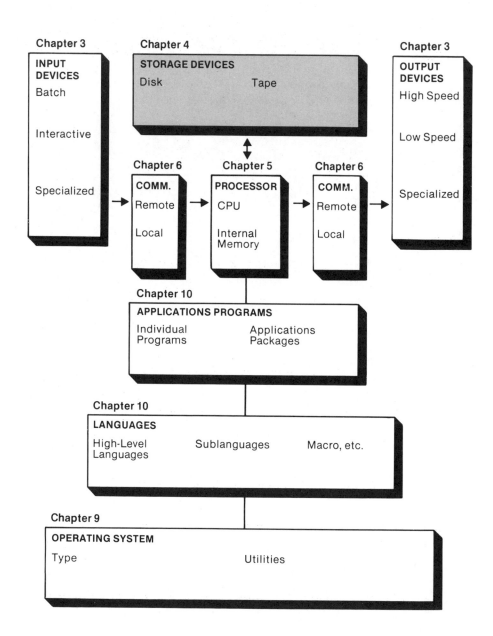

Chapter 3

INPUT DEVICES

Batch

Interactive

Specialized

Chapter 4

STORAGE DEVICES

Disk   Tape

Chapter 3

OUTPUT DEVICES

High Speed

Low Speed

Specialized

Chapter 6

COMM.

Remote

Local

Chapter 5

PROCESSOR

CPU

Internal Memory

Chapter 6

COMM.

Remote

Local

Chapter 10

APPLICATIONS PROGRAMS

Individual Programs   Applications Packages

Chapter 10

LANGUAGES

High-Level Languages   Sublanguages   Macro, etc.

Chapter 9

OPERATING SYSTEM

Type   Utilities

Computers and the Elephantine Memory Problem

It was six men of Hindustan,
To learning much inclined,
Who went to see the elephant,
(Though all of them were blind);
That each by observation
Might satisfy his mind.

The first approached the elephant,
And happening to fall
Against his broad and sturdy side,
At once began to bawl,
"Bless me, it seems the elephant
Is very like a wall."

. . .

The sixth no sooner had begun
About the beast to grope
Than, seizing on the swinging tail
That fell within his scope,
"I see," cried he, "the elephant
Is very like a rope."

And so these men of Hindustan
Disputed loud and long,
Each of his own opinion
Exceeding stiff and strong,
Though each was partly in the right,
And all were in the wrong!

— John Godfrey Saxe

Like the Hindustani sages in their encounter with the elephant, our brief and limited contacts with computer systems can give us misleading impressions about the kinds of modern technology available for "remembering" huge amounts of data in the computer. The computer, like the elephant of children's books, is supposed never to forget — at least, until we tell it to forget. What are those devices that empower a computer system to become a "memory bank"? Collectively, they are simply called "memory."

INTERNAL AND SECONDARY MEMORY

At the present time there is no one memory device that is all things to all applications of a computer system; different kinds of devices have been developed to meet different needs.

The first distinction we must make is between primary and secondary storage. Primary memory is the very high-speed memory intimately associated with the processor or central processing unit (CPU). Secondary memory refers to the **mass storage devices** available.

In the computer's **internal memory**, programs and data are temporarily stored and made immediately available for processing. The overriding needs here are for higher speed and **random access**, which means that any part of memory may be **read**, or **accessed**, equally quickly. Numerous kinds of internal memory have been developed, each one usually faster and cheaper than its predecessor. Existing machines use magnetic core memory (made up of tiny donuts of magnetic material), or various kinds of large-scale integration (LSI) electronic **semiconductor memory** devices that are not unlike transistors. Notable over the past few years has been a trend toward extreme miniaturization, and consequently, dramatically reduced cost. The minicomputers available today cost far less than their predecessors, and boast much larger **memory sizes** of 64 K (64×2^{10}) **words** and more.

Most internal memory is used transiently. For instance, data is kept in the machine only while a program is running and is then overwritten by the next program. More recently, developments in LSI circuitry such as the **read only memory** (**ROM**) and variations on this theme have changed the role of internal memory. It is more common today to find programs or data stored permanently in ROMs in computer-based instruments. These programs are not available for user modification.

Internal memory, however, is relatively costly per character, and therefore the amount of internal memory will always be limited. Since computers must process vast quantities of data, there must be economical ways of storing that data in computer-accessible form. Various secondary memory technologies serve that purpose.

Figure 4.1 details the differing price/performance characteristics of various secondary memories. It should be noted that the ulti-

	Capacity (in bytes)	Cost of drive*	Cost of media	If on-line, approximate access
Cassettes	100–300Kb	Dual: $3000–$5000	$6–$20	20 sec
Reel tapes 800BPI:	10Mb	$7000–$20,000	$14	Seconds–minutes
6250BPI:	125Mb	$13,000–$31,000	$17	Seconds–minutes
Mini-diskettes	90–125Kb	Single: $1100	$5–$7	400 msec
Diskettes (floppy disks)	250Kb–1Mb	Single: $3000 Dual: $5000	$6–$10	400 msec
Head-per-track	256Kb–20Mb	$10,000–$67,000	N/A	8–17 msec
Cartridge disks	2–5Mb	$5000–$10,000	$80–$120	17 msec
Disk packs Small:	5–90Mb	$10,000–$40,000	$100–$1000	17 msec
Large:	100–400Mb	$15,000–$65,000	$800–$4000	30–60 msec
Terabit (mass storage systems)	3.–1Tb	$500,000–	–	1–10 sec

*As part of a computer system from a typical company.

Fig. 4.1. Secondary memory devices

mate economy of a storage device will be determined by the average cost *for each character* stored on-line. Figure 4.2 shows the relationships between speed and cost on the one hand, and speed and capacity on the other among all types of memory devices. Internal storage is more expensive, but faster; secondary (mass) storage is cheaper, but slower. Each device fills a unique niche in the price/performance spectrum. We shall examine each of the secondary memory technologies more closely.

Secondary memory devices fall into two categories: sequential devices and random-access devices.

Sequential devices permit information to be written onto or read off some storage **medium** in a fixed sequence only. In order to get at a particular data item, it is necessary to pass over all the data preceding it. Low cost is the hallmark of sequential-memory technologies such as the well-known magnetic tape. On the other hand, access to specified data may take a considerable length of time.

The so-called "random-access" devices are designed to permit direct, or almost direct (**pseudo-random**), access to specified data. These devices bypass large amounts of irrelevant data and thereby reduce access time considerably. Magnetic disks exemplify this kind of technology. They are much faster than tape systems, but they are also more expensive.

MAGNETIC TAPE

In 1953, half-inch reels of magnetic tape became available commercially, and this width has since become the industry standard. Today's tapes are composed of a strong plastic backing coated on one side with magnetizable material. (Any secondary memory device that uses a magnetic material to record data is called a **magnetic memory** device.) Tapes are normally kept **off-line** (not mounted on a tape drive connected to a computer) in libraries, and they are loaded, usually by a human operator, onto **drives** only when the data or the programs they contain are needed. Reels are usually 2400 feet long and the amount of data stored on a reel varies tremendously among various tape drives. Although drives commonly record information at a density of 800 or 1600 bits per inch (BPI), the newest units can record at 6250 BPI. At that density, a 2400-foot reel can hold ap-

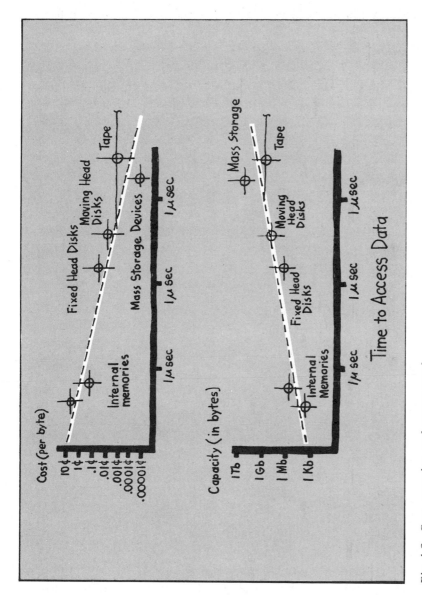

Fig. 4.2. Cost, capacity, and access speed

These two graphs summarize the rationale for having many kinds of memory, and they show the trade-offs that must be made. In general, higher-capacity memories cost less per character stored — as long as one pays the penalty of slower access time. Choosing the mix is one of the tricks. The bars represent the approximate ranges of data; there are rather broad limits. (Adapted from D. J. Theis, An overview of memory technologies, *Datamation* 24: 114–115, 1978; and J. A. Rajchman, New memory technologies, *Science* 195: 1228, 1977.)

proximately 1/8 billion (125 million) characters (or **bytes**) of information. Most tape drives today store data in nine parallel **tracks** oriented lengthwise. Each character is **written** by a set of magnetic recording heads (one for each track; see Fig. 4.3a) across the tape, one bit per track (nine-track format; see Fig. 4.3b). Some older drives use a seven-track format.

Tape drive controllers write and read data onto magnetic tape in chunks, or "blocks." The amount of space left between these blocks (inter-record gap) to allow starting or stopping the tape will influence the amount of information that a tape can hold.

The read/write speed of tape drives varies considerably. Some units are as slow as 25 inches per second (IPS), while others achieve speeds of 200 IPS or more. Magnetic tape is the slowest storage medium in terms of access to the data. At 25 IPS it would take $(12 \times 2400) \div 25 = 1152$ seconds or 19.2 minutes simply to read a 2400-foot tape from end to end non-stop! Magnetic tape is therefore best suited for storing information that is either organized sequentially or accessed only occasionally. Because magnetic tape is such an inexpensive medium, it is an attractive choice for archival storage of large quantities of information. When data manipulation has been completed in the computer, results are often dumped onto tape. The next time a program user needs the data on the tape, it may be read directly or transferred onto high-speed devices such as disks. In this way, the high cost of **on-line** storage on more expensive media between runs is eliminated.

Tape is probably the medium most transportable between different systems, although there are incompatibilities that sometimes frustrate such attempts. When transportability is essential, equipment and software compatibility must be scrutinized carefully.

Cassettes and tape cartridges are interesting developments in tape media. Most are like the familiar music cassette. This medium is a slow, low-capacity, but cheap way to store from 100K to 256K characters (although larger-capacity cartridges do exist), and has found favor in intelligent terminals and some microcomputer systems.

Finally, a variety of special tape systems are available, one of which is fairly familiar: the **LINC** tape or **DEC** tape. These

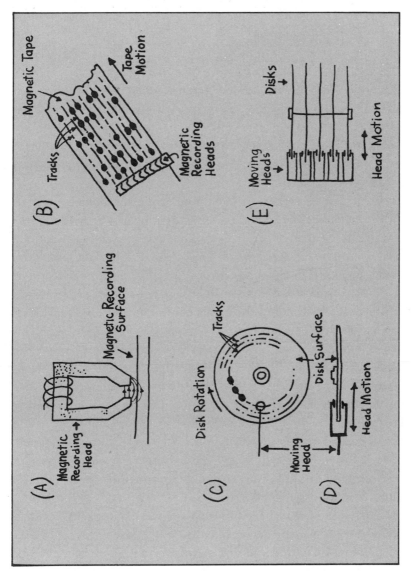

Fig. 4.3. **Magnetic recording devices**
(a) Magnetic recording head. (b) How digital data is recorded on nine-track magnetic tape; storing a 1 is indicated by a black mark. (c) Magnetic disk, top view. (d) Magnetic disk, side view. (e) Disk pack of five platters with ganged moving heads.

small, wide tapes are somewhat like slow linear "disks" in that data is stored in fixed physical locations. They hold only about 300K characters.

DISKS FOR EVERYONE

Magnetic disk storage was developed to accommodate the need for a fast, near-random access, high-capacity secondary storage medium. Disks come in many sizes and types. The two main types are rigid disks and flexible disks. Rigid disks come in two forms: moving-head and fixed-head. Moving-head disks are further divided into cartridge and pack varieties.

Disk cartridges contain a single circular platter, coated on both sides with a magnetizable material. The cartridge can be loaded onto a drive that spins the disk at high speed. The drive provides retractable heads that fly on a thin layer of air above the disk surface. Information is read and written by the recording heads, one for each side of the disk. The information is written in concentric circles called tracks on the surface of the disk and the heads can move radially from track to track. (See Fig. 4.3c, d, e.)

When a number of disk platters are stacked one above the other on a common spindle, the configuration is called a disk pack. Each platter is the same as in the case of the cartridge, but in the drive the heads are ganged together and move as a unit, accessing a whole stack of tracks (called a **cylinder**) on the pack at once. The capacity of disks depends on the recording density. Density is measured in terms of both the number of tracks and the amount of data in each track. One hundred Mbyte packs are not uncommon today; some packs even hold up to 500 Mbytes.

Recently, there has been a move toward "datapacks" — disk packs with the moving heads sealed inside the pack. Sealed packs reduce the deleterious effects of dirt and dust on high-density recording media. The cost of the pack itself is substantially (three to five times) greater than conventional disk packs, but the drives are often less expensive than alternatives.

For very fast access, some disk drives feature a single nonremovable platter with multiple fixed heads. Instead of a single head that is moved to access each track, one of these fixed heads is permanently positioned over each track. A slightly higher-speed predecessor of the fixed-head disk, the magnetic drum, is still found in some older, larger installations. Drums also have one head per track, but the tracks appear in an equatorial pattern on the cylindrical surface. Modern semiconductor technology is supplanting these expensive devices.

Most of the rigid disk media (packs or cartridges) accessed by moving heads can be physically removed from their drives and placed off-line in a library, whence they can be recalled and remounted when required. Thus, the same drive can use many disk packs, just as one tape drive can read from or write on any number of tape reels. Interestingly, one survey showed that the number of packs per drive averages 1.1; i.e., there is only one pack in the library for every ten packs permanently on drives. Either the information kept on random-access disks is too important to be taken off-line at any time, or the on-line capacity of disk-pack technology is adequate for the storage needs of the average installation. In any event, the feature of removability does not appear to be as important for big disk packs with the result that less expensive, nonremovable disk-pack drives have become available. Single platter disk cartridges are usually an exception to this observation, because their total capacity (two to five Mbytes) is so small that off-line capacity is important.

An intriguing form of disk technology is the **floppy disk** or **diskette**, which because of its low cost has found tremendous acceptance in the microcomputer marketplace. The diskette itself costs from six to ten dollars, and a drive that will hold two on-line diskettes usually costs under $5000. A single-density, single-sided diskette can hold about 250K characters of information. Double-density, double-sided diskettes will hold about 1,000,000 (1M) characters of data. A smaller version of the floppy disk, the "mini-diskette," holds about 90K characters in a format similar to full-sized diskettes. The floppy disk is the cheapest kind of pseudo-random access storage available. Its principal drawback is slow access time.

Diskettes are very manageable media. They are relatively durable and they can be sent through the mail or filed in ordinary folders.

For this reason they are attractive for those kinds of applications in which data is collected from several remote locations and sent to a central computer.

As you see, disk technology comes in a wide range of capacities, speeds, and costs. There are disks to serve all types of users, from the computer hobbyist to the largest multimillion-dollar corporation that needs the kind of computer installation that can store huge quantities of data.

PRODIGIOUS MEMORIES

The desire to provide enormous permanent storage capacity at the lowest possible price per character stored has led to the development of a few extraordinary mass storage devices. One company markets a fully automatic tape library capable of mechanically loading, threading, and unloading any of 7000 standard tape reels. It does this under computer control, without human intervention. Several companies manufacture mass memories whose capacities range from .3 to several trillion (1,000,000 million or 10^{12}) characters, and these are called **terabyte memories**. These mass storage devices feature strips of wide magnetic tape that are automatically loaded and unloaded from read-write drives as required. One device employs videotape on which digital information is stored at high density. Research in photo-optical (holographic) techniques for even higher capacity is under way. All of these devices cost half a million dollars or more, and are thus out of the reach of all but the most giant, centralized applications.

OTHER OFF-LINE STORAGE MEDIA

Although punched cards and paper tape have been generally superseded as secondary storage media, they still offer unique characteristics that are utilized from time to time.

These media are emotionally reassuring. There is something real and satisfying about visible holes in pieces of paper. The fact that people can read data printed at the top of punched cards is a plus. However, paper media have very low storage density — only 80 characters on a whole card, for example.

Unlike many magnetic media, though, cards and paper tape are standard enough in format so that they are transportable among different systems. In some instances this is a great asset. Very small amounts of data requiring only rare transaction with computers can be stored on cards or on specialized media such as magnetic strip cards the size of common credit cards.

THE ELEPHANT'S GRAVEYARD

The bones of many mastodons litter the evolutionary trail of computer-memory technology. Advancing technology has superseded many earlier devices. Moreover, as various types of memories have decreased in cost and grown in capacity, they have gradually absorbed roles previously relegated to other devices.

The series of increasingly sophisticated internal memory devices, each one supplanting its predecessors, has included relays, vacuum tubes, electromechanical delay lines, electron beam devices, magnetic drums, magnetic core memory, and semiconductor memory.

Conceptually, the current semiconductor revolution is a throwback to the vacuum tube or at least to its replacement, the transistor. However, large-scale integration has made these newer memories much smaller, cheaper, and less hungry for power than the behemoths of yore. Semiconductors have progressed rapidly toward greater reliability, higher speed, and ever greater miniaturization.

Two of the newer memory innovations are magnetic bubble memories and charge coupled devices (CCDs), each competing to fill the cost-performance gap between disks and faster internal memory. If successful, these technologies will replace fixed-head disks because they offer more speed and greater capacity at a lower price.

In an environment of constant technical upheaval, some secondary storage devices are necessarily doomed to failure even from their very inception. A mass storage device called the "data cell," for instance, used strips of magnetic tape that were pulled from a rack to be read or written. This device was never sufficiently reliable to catch on, and before all its wrinkles had been ironed out, it was superseded by more reliable devices of larger capacity.

Research continues on memory technologies that will someday make current devices obsolete. Ironically, several old technologies such as electron beam memories, taking advantage of modern electronics and more sophisticated fabrication techniques, may make comebacks.

A WARNING

The care and feeding of elephants is so expensive that these beasts are seldom kept as pets. Usually they have to earn their keep. On the other hand, the occasional temple elephant is maintained in idle splendor. The computer world has its equivalent — mass storage dedicated to unused data.

One pays heavily in order to let data live in computer memory devices. This charge is painfully apparent to users who pay for on-line disk storage in a time-sharing system. At the end of each month a bill is received, based on the amount of storage used. Many other "taxes" are involved; the investment in software development and maintenance that permits one to use a computer for anything is substantial. When one elects to pay these taxes, there should be a good reason for doing so: It should be truly necessary to keep data in a computer system. One would imagine this observation to be self-evident, but in fact the point is sometimes missed.

To serve users who put data into computers for reasons other than for information processing — prestige, make-work projects, etc. — computer scientists have invented the tongue-in-cheek concept of Write-Only Memory, or WOM (pronounced "wahm"). You can stuff data into WOM, but you can never read it back again. It is the perfect place for unused data. Since WOM does not need to "recall" anything, its inventors assure us that it is dirt cheap. It is the ideal means to achieve the aura of sophistication associated with being "computerized" without tying up much money in the process.

There is a serious moral. It warns us against salting away unused data for a rainy day or for the sake of keeping up with the Babbages.

Only rich temples can afford to keep a White Elephant.

THE END OF THE TALE

The blind men of Hindustan could not appreciate the holistic nature of their subject, the elephant. They argued "loud and long," each one expounding his own limited impression.

We are more fortunate. In examining how our electronic elephant never forgets, we have learned that although computer memory technology comes in many guises, no one type is necessarily *the* correct or best one. Each device has proved useful in particular circumstances. In any computer application, memory devices are selected on the basis of their differing capacity, price, speed, and other characteristics in order to meet specific needs. The good system designer never makes the mistake of the Hindustani sages, but knows instead that a blend, sometimes of many memory technologies, is necessary in a system. The good system designer perceives that a useful whole is made up of well-selected parts.

In a complex area such as computer memory systems it is difficult to be an enlightened consumer. But if you are, you will have two advantages. First, to a limited extent, you will be able to "look over the shoulder" of system developers and ask them the right questions about what they are doing or have done. More importantly, knowing the constraints of memory technology, you will be in a position to assist a developer by expressing your needs in a realistic manner.

BIBLIOGRAPHY

Internal Memory

Bowers, D. M., Magnetic core memories — a tutorial review. *Modern Data* 8:8:51 (August) 1975.

Hodges, D. A., Microelectronic memories. *Scientific American* 237:9:130 (September) 1977.

Stiefel, M. L., (Add on) memories are made of this. *Mini-Micro Systems* 10:6:35 (June) 1977.

Tapes

Caswell, S. A., Tape cartridge drives and systems. *Modern Data* 8:9:25 (September) 1975.

Moritz, F. G., Conventional magnetic tape equipment. *Modern Data* 8:3:51 (March) 1975.

Disks

Bowers, D. M., Floppy disk drives and systems. *Mini-Micro Systems* 10:2:36 (February) 1977.

Brechtlein, R., Comparing disk technologies. *Datamation* 24:1:139 (January) 1978.

Sollman, G. H., A guide to floppy disk selection. *Mini-Micro Systems* 10:4:36 (April) 1977.

General Tutorial

Theis, D. J., An overview of memory technologies. *Datamation* 24:1:113 (January) 1978.

Miscellaneous New Devices

Cashman, M. W., A read/write optical memory system. *Datamation* 19:3:66 (March) 1973.

Jamieson, J. M., The CCD memory gains a foothold. *Mini-Micro Systems* 10:4:18 (April) 1977.

The outlook for bubble memory devices. *Mini-Micro Systems* 11:2:32 (February) 1978.

NEW WORDS

access	memory size
byte	off-line
cylinder	on-line
diskette	pseudo-random access memory
drive	RAM, *R*andom *A*ccess *M*emory
floppy disk	random access, *see* RAM
Gb (Gigabyte)	read
internal memory	ROM, *R*ead *O*nly *M*emory
Kb (Kilobyte)	semiconductor memory
K, Kilo	sequential access memory
magnetic memory	Tb (Terabyte)
mass storage device	track
Mb (Megabyte)	word
medium	write

5

The Origin of the Species

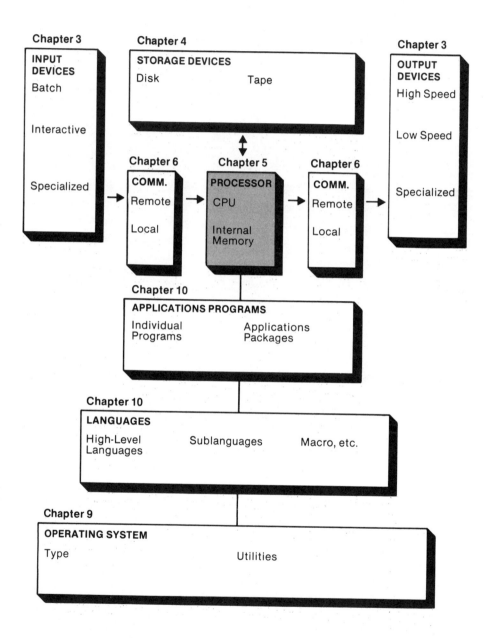

The Central Processing Unit

Up to this point we have considered the peripheral parts that make up a computer system: devices for input and output, and the various memory technologies for storing data. Now let us look at the very heart of any computer system — the central processing unit, or CPU.

THE STRUCTURE OF PROCESSORS

In common parlance, the words "computer" and "processor" are frequently used interchangeably. More properly, "computer" refers to the central processing unit plus internal memory. The CPU alone is the **processor,** and this is the device to which we now turn our attention.

In **digital computers** the processor can be dissected into two functional units: the **control unit** and the **arithmetic unit.**

The control unit is that portion of the computer that interprets the program instructions and directs the sequence of operations determined by the instructions.

The arithmetic unit is that portion of computer hardware in which arithmetic (add, subtract, multiply, divide) and logical operations (true-false, and, or , not, exclusive or) are performed under the direction of the control unit. The arithmetic unit has its own very high-speed memory units called **registers** in which operands (items of data to be manipulated) and results are placed during arithmetic processing.

Programs and the data on which they operate must be in internal memory in order to be processed. Thus, if located on secondary memory devices such as disk or tape, programs and data are first loaded into internal memory.

Programs are made up of the **instructions** (or operations) of which a given computer is capable. Programmers write programs in various programming languages (such as assembler or FORTRAN), and these in turn are translated by other system programs into the proper combination of the machine's internal instructions (machine language). We will have more to say about programming and software in Part III. Each machine instruction is represented by a number, usually binary. When instructions are to be **executed** — that is, carried out — they are put into successive internal memory locations.

A memory location will hold one number of the appropriate bit length for the machine. This number might be either one machine-language instruction or a data item, depending only on the context in which it is used. Each memory location has an **address**, a unique number associated with each memory location in the computer.

To execute a program, the control unit must find the first instruction; to do this, it must know at what location the first instruction to be executed in the program can be found. Starting there, the CPU gets from each successive location the instruction contained therein, interprets the instruction, and performs the sequence of operations that the instruction represents. The control unit continues getting instructions from the next sequential location, unless it encounters instructions that tell it to get instructions from other locations. By analogy, it is rather like going from one house to the next and doing what each occupant tells you to do, until you discover someone who tells you to skip the next five houses or to go to another street.

When an instruction is encountered that involves an arithmetic or logical operation, the arithmetic unit will be called into action, in much the same way that a person might resort to a calculator while in the process of solving a mathematical problem. When the arithmetic operation is complete the results are tucked away in some location for later use and the program continues, directed by the control unit.

The basic parts and fundamental machine-language instructions of a computer are simple. Yet when orchestrated by the proper program they are like the strings of a guitar or the keys of a piano: an infinity of possibilities results.

HUMBLE BEGINNINGS?

The crude mechanical antecedents of computers are interesting, but the first electronic machine that at least vaguely resembled contemporary computers appeared in the 1940s.

As it turns out, the beginnings of the modern electronic computer were far from humble. The first useful computers were huge, complex machines for calculation and message deciphering, developed through vastly expensive military projects during World War II. [1] These devices and their immediate descendents stretched relay and vacuum-tube technology to their limits in order to realize useful circuitry. In sheer bulk and physical impressiveness, the first electronic computers resembled our concept of the fearsome "Big Brother." However, there was little danger that they would take over anything, because for all their bulk they were dumb and their capacity for storing and processing data was small. The enormous expense and the difficulty of assembling such one-of-a-kind machines assured that they would be limited to specific important tasks. Despite their limitations these machines were successful as stupendous calculators, computing such things as projectile trajectories for military purposes.

Modern-day computers inherit this capability as calculators, but they are still poor at other tasks — notably those functions that we commonly regard as "intelligent."

So impressed were people by the calculating ability of the first computers that they felt that four or five such machines could probably handle the whole world's needs. [2] Thus began the human tendency to extrapolate the impact of computers beyond their real capabilities and to misinterpret the true depth and breadth of computing needs in the world.

Fueled and benefited by the microelectronics revolution, computers have evolved substantially in the past three decades. California's "Silicon Valley" (the nickname for the place where most of the American semiconductor industry is located) is to the electronics revolution what the Olduvai Gorge is to paleontology. Picking through some of its artifacts, one observer in a recent issue of *Scientific American* explained just how far we have advanced:

> Today's microcomputer, at a cost of perhaps $300, has more computing capacity than the first large electronic computer, ENIAC. It is 20 times faster, has a larger memory, is thousands of times more reliable, consumes the power of a light-

bulb rather than a locomotive, occupies 1/30,000 the volume and costs 1/10,000 as much. It is available by mail order or at your local hobby shop. [3]

The vector of evolution during this time has been toward high-density, low-cost computing power. We are beginning to achieve mass availability. Computers, like the animals of the earth, have grown in ability and number.

SMALL, MEDIUM, AND LARGE COMPUTERS

Many of today's computers are more sophisticated than those of 20 years ago and cover a wide range of capabilities and prices. Therefore, a computer must be carefully chosen from the large selection in order to meet particular needs.

It is convenient to classify today's computers into general categories. One commonly thinks of micro-, mini-, midi-, maxi-, and "super"computers. As technology progresses inexorably, today's "large" computer (powerful, expensive, and often physically big) becomes tomorrow's "smaller" computer (powerful, cheaper, and physically small). The biggest machines of tomorrow will have capabilities far beyond yesterday's best.

The most exciting development of recent years has been the **microprocessor**. One can discern a gradual but predictable evolution toward the microprocessor over the last 25 years. The trend toward modularization (the use of relatively few kinds of boards interconnected to form complete subsystems), came to commercial fruition in the late 1950s and early 1960s. At that time, computers made up of multiple modules, each module holding many transistors, became commonplace. A significant advance quietly took place in the early 1970s when it became possible to construct a whole central processing unit with the use of integrated circuits or ICs (each equivalent to about 100 transistors) that fit on a single, rather large module or card. Finally, the step of placing a whole processor on a single semiconductor chip — not much larger than the earliest transistors — was taken in the last few years. The microprocessor had arrived. Each such microprocessor chip contains the equivalent of several thousand transistors.

Fig. 5.1.   Will the real "Big Brother" please stand up?

Each day, yesterday's marvel is outdone as greater and greater miniaturization packs more and more powerful processors and more memory into the same space, thereby greatly reducing the cost of fabrication. Today, whole processors can be soldered into place on a board in the amount of time and space formerly dedicated to a lone transistor (Fig. 5.2).

The implication of physically small, inexpensive, yet powerful computers is evident. Instruments and equipment of all kinds can now contain a computer, and can benefit from this revolution. Instruments can be more adept at manipulating and transforming data, and can quickly give us final results instead of partial results that we must then turn into useful parameters. Adapting instruments becomes far more reasonable, since expensive rewiring or complete redesign is replaced by reprogramming.

The modularity derived from small, less expensive instruments means that growth can be accommodated by adding additional units rather than by trading in a whole system for a more powerful one. Today's microprocessors cost only a few tens or hundreds of dollars. Complete, usable microcomputer systems (CPU, memory, disks, printer) can cost about ten thousand dollars, but they are getting cheaper.

Although microcomputers are very limited in terms of sophisticated numeric computation ("number crunching"), they are often adequate for the type of calculation and data management functions important in business applications.

At the next stratum of complexity, the **minicomputer** system usually costs from a few thousand dollars to $250,000 or more, of which the processor itself represents only a small portion (in the range of 5%–25%) of the total cost. In return for this substantial investment, one obtains a machine with more overall power than many of the largest computers of two decades ago. Minicomputers today are suitable for simultaneous use by even tens of users; for database management; for many small computer-based products; and for limited computation-oriented functions. The word "limited" should not be misinterpreted. Although minicomputers are generally unsuitable for solving complex sets of equations quickly, they can

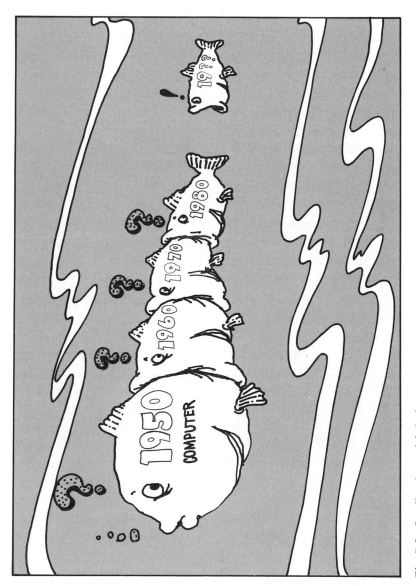

Fig. 5.2. Smaller, but mightier!

solve the sophisticated problem of reconstructing complex medical x-ray images in seconds to minutes. In very specialized areas such as signal processing, they can be augmented by special processing units (Fourier or array processors) and are then capable of solving computationally heavy problems in fractions of a second.

Information processing in medicine has already benefited immensely from minicomputer technology because of the relatively low cost of these machines. The first major breakthrough was the LINC processor, developed during the 1960s under the auspices of the National Institutes of Health. [4] This prototypal unit was integrated into a number of commercial computers (the LINC-8, the PC-12, etc.) and served as the stimulus for much computing development. Many commercial products running the programs developed for these earlier machines are still extant.

There are many minicomputers available commercially. A recent survey listed 38 companies selling 95 models — numbers that are definitely underestimates. [5]

Today the power of minicomputers is being extended by using microcomputers as peripheral processors or controllers. By "unloading" the central minicomputer of simple but time-consuming data management operations, these controllers can create a faster, more efficient computer system. A logical extension has been to unburden the system of low-speed user-oriented interaction by using intelligent terminals for data collection and editing. In this operation, a processor is put in each terminal and the central computer is interrupted only when blocks of correctly formatted and validated data have been assembled.

The distinction between micro- and minicomputers may disappear in the near future. More powerful micros are even now surpassing older minis. It is also possible that arrays of microprocessors may take over functions now assigned to much larger single computers. The "Hypercube" is a commercially available, expandable processor made of modular microprocessor segments. This may signal the wave of the future.

Occasionally the most powerful minicomputers and the bottom end of the line of maxicomputers are classed together and called **midicomputers.** [6] One source has defined them as machines with word-lengths of 24 or 32 bits. We will not deal separately with these here.

Throughout the entire spectrum from micro- to maxicomputers, more powerful computers differ from less powerful machines in several ways. More powerful machines have a larger repertoire of more complex instructions, and they can execute these instructions more quickly. The longer word size of "larger" machines permits a bigger instruction set, access to more memory in a single step, and more rapid large-number arithmetic. Whereas "smaller" computers may take several steps to perform some given operation, a "larger" machine may accomplish the same thing with one instruction. Moving upward through this spectrum one will find the increasing use of peripheral processors to unload the main computer of input/output functions.

Micro- and most minicomputers have only one **channel** connecting disk to computer, and this may be quite slow. The largest minicomputers and larger machines introduce parallelism, a method by which several channels are available for simultaneous data movement, with each channel itself able to transfer more data. The more powerful computers also make use of very high-speed supplementary main memories (cache memories) into which data and programs to be imminently dealt with are transferred for very rapid access. Some computers can even execute parts or all of several instructions simultaneously. These internal architectural features are apparent to the user as very much higher execution speeds, or to use an industry term, as higher throughput.

Maxicomputer systems — or mainframes — are those incorporating some or all of these features and are most suitable for big, centralized applications. They are appropriate for the processing of immense amounts of data. Research of many types may also benefit from maxicomputer systems — for instance, mathematical modeling of physiologic systems or even of national budgets or world economy.

There are a few notable **supercomputers**. Each of these is essentially an experiment in computer architecture costing millions of dollars. The goal in developing these systems is to create machines that can execute many operations in parallel, thus achieving previously impossible speeds.

THE COMPUTER IN CONTEXT

A bare CPU is relatively inexpensive, but useless. The CPU in a $100,000 minicomputer system may cost only $5000, with memory generally adding about $20,000 more. The remaining 75 percent of the cost is made up of the peripheral devices that transfigure the naked computer into a usable computer system.

A computer system does not stand alone. Just as the CPU requires peripheral devices, so a computer system must be placed in an environment tailored to its requirements. Numerous factors must be considered.

Computers generate heat. Each six-foot high rack develops at least a few thousand BTUs. Large computers generate so much heat that they have internal cooling systems, including refrigeration and water-cooling schemes. Almost any room intended to house something larger than a small microcomputer system needs air-conditioning.

While microcomputer systems can plug into the standard wall-power outlet, many minicomputers require special plugs and higher currents than usually available. Big machines often have peculiar power and voltage requirements. Uninterruptable power supplies are needed to keep essential computers operational in the face of "brownouts" and power failures.

Security for expensive computer systems holding private information includes physical measures such as locks on the door, limited access to the facilities, and controlled access to terminals. There must also be protection against fire. Fire-extinguishing gas must be installed in the computer area, since water is as damaging as flames to electronics and storage media.

The physical bulk of a computer system may, in some cases, dictate where it can be used. Housing very large computer systems can tie up expensive floor space.

Of course, computers are worthless without the people who maintain and program them. Personnel represent a large hidden cost in a computer operation.

WHAT'S NEXT?

Computers have progressed a very long way since the days when they were all multimillion-dollar monsters. There are still huge and expensive computers, but their power was unimaginable in the early days of computer history. Today, sophisticated computer systems are available at prices nearly every enterprise can afford. Even the consumer who can afford a stereo system can purchase a computer more powerful than the legendary ENIAC of not too many years ago. The proliferation of hobby computers in the consumer domain guarantees that the computer will become even more available, easier to use, and less mysterious. Therefore, computers are moving toward becoming simply another tool — and a pervasive one at that (Fig. 5.3).

NOTES

1. A. C. Brown, *Bodyguard of Lies.* New York: Bantam, 1975.

2. R. N. Noyce, Microelectronics. *Scientific American* 237:9:62 (September) 1977.

3. Ibid., p. 65.

4. W. A. Clark, and C. E. Molnar, Description of the LINC. In *Computers in Biomedical Research*, edited by R. W. Stacy and B. D. Waxman, New York: Academic Press, Vol. 2, 1965, pp. 35-66.

5. Advancing technology yields more and better minicomputers. *Canadian Datasystems* 9:7:38 (July) 1977.

6. D. J. Theis, The midicomputer. *Datamation* 23:2:73 (February) 1977.

BIBLIOGRAPHY

Modern Processors

Advancing technology yields more and better minicomputers. *Canadian Datasystems* 9:7:38 (July) 1977.

Ogdin, C. A., Microcomputer overview (8 chapters). *Mini-Micro Systems* 10:11:32 (November) 1977.

Sutherland, I. E., and C. A. Mead, Microelectronics and computer science. *Scientific American* 237:9:210 (September) 1977.

Terman, L. M., The role of microelectronics in data processing. *Scientific American* 237:9:162 (September) 1977.

Toong, H. M. D., Microprocessors. *Scientific American* 237:9:146 (September) 1977.

History

Grosch, H. R. J., The way it was — 1957. *Datamation* 23:9:75 (September) 1977.

Fig. 5.3.
Originality in the application of computers in any area is increasingly found with the professionals in that field.

Hushey, H. D., Chronology of computing devices. *IEEE Transactions on Computers*, C-25:1190 (December) 1976.

Myers, W., Key developments in computer technology. *Computer* 9:11:48 (November) 1976.

NEW WORDS

address	maxicomputer
arithmetic unit	microprocessor
channel	midicomputer
control unit	minicomputer
digital computer	processor
execute	register
instruction	supercomputer
mainframe	

6

The Missing Link

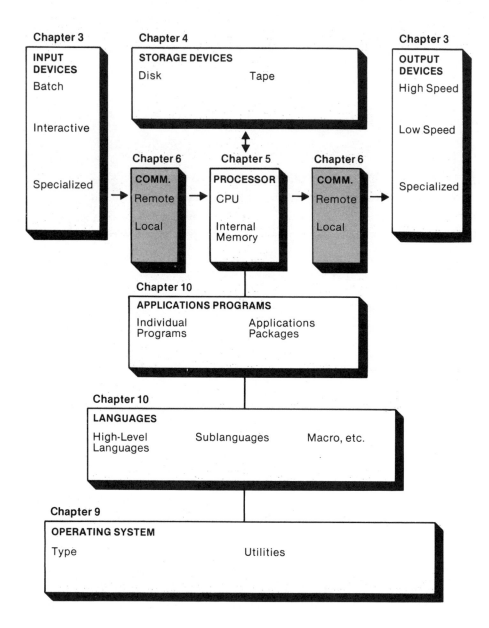

Communications Devices

The hardware of computer systems includes central processing units, storage devices, and equipment for input and output. We have discussed these sorts of equipment in the preceding chapters. There remains, however, the question of how the various pieces of hardware communicate with each other. The answer is simple: through communication devices.

Unfortunately, communications technology has a low profile. Millions of people who use telephones never give a second thought to the intricate system that makes their conversations possible. Even among computer professionals communications is not a high-awareness topic, perhaps because of the relative strangeness of the underlying technology. Whatever the reasons, this topic is ignored or skipped over in many discussions about computer hardware.

Such an omission is serious, for the effects of ignoring communications problems can be fatal for a project.

A failure to study the real communications needs in an application of computers will almost certainly result in a project that will run aground. When limited understanding leads to merely automating paths of communications that have been established by tradition, a storm is looming on the horizon. Furthermore, selecting inappropriate devices and media may severely limit the usefulness of computer systems in which they are used. You know the trip is over when the resultant communications system is unacceptably expensive in proportion to its limited usefulness.

There is no need for this kind of disaster, since a systematic study can determine what pathways of communications should be established on the basis of real need. With this study in hand and a knowledge of alternative technologies, it is possible to chart a safe course and to create an efficient, economical system.

The complexity and the unfamiliarity of the devices involved make this an area in which the developers of computer systems must make careful and informed decisions. This complexity and unfamiliarity lead even experienced computer system developers to seek advice from experts when designing systems in which communications technology is a prime factor. Therefore, as a user of computer systems you cannot expect to be your own expert. Yet, by being aware of the problems and some of the available solutions, you will at least know when a developer has done the necessary homework, and you will therefore be less likely to be fooled into accepting expedience as necessity or into crediting cheap and inadequate solutions.

MOVING DATA FROM PLACE TO PLACE

There are two basic ways of moving data from point to point: in parallel or in serial.

High-speed devices such as disks, magnetic tape drives and most line printers are connected to the computer via **parallel interfaces.** Interfacing in parallel means that an entire word of data has its component bits (usually 16 bits or more) moved simultaneously between the computer and the device along 16 or more parallel wires — one wire for each bit plus others for control signals. In this way, huge rates of data transfer are realized. For example, disks may send 1,000,000 words per second to the processor. At these rates, signal delays and distortion caused by excessive lengths of cable could cause parallel-interfaced equipment to malfunction. Therefore disks, tapes, line printers, and other high-speed devices must be located close to the computer. There is seldom any choice. These high-speed devices plug into the central processing unit. The multiwire cables interconnecting them run within the system cabinets or beneath the raised floor of the computer room. The links are not really "missing": they are just hidden.

On the other hand, when remote terminals must gain access to a computer, or when two or more geographically separate computer systems must communicate, a different approach is indicated for both technical and economic reasons. To achieve economical digital communications in this case, data is transmitted in serial mode — one bit at a time — utilizing as few wires as possible. A variety of communications media ranging from wires to light "pipes" exist to support serial communications. Serial-communications interfaces (**serial interfaces**) perform the task of sending the bits that make up a character (or word) one bit at a time, and of reassembling the bits at the receiving end into characters (or words).

SERIAL COMMUNICATIONS METHODS

To conceptualize this method, we will imagine that we are attempting to communicate over a wire between two points. (See Fig. 6.1.) Digital data can be represented on this wire by two voltage levels: for example, a positive voltage can represent a "one" and zero volts (or ground) can represent zero. Each one or zero is a bit, and combinations of ones and zeros make up the codes for characters. Thus what we have is somewhat like Morse Code, except we use high and low voltages instead of dashes and dots to represent characters. There are two methods for achieving serial digital communications: asynchronous and synchronous.

Asynchronous Method

In **asynchronous** communications, characters are transmitted (or received) with an arbitrary time between each of them — for example, one character is sent whenever a user hits a key on the keyboard of the terminal. Each transmitted character has one "start bit" and one or two "stop bits" added to the beginning and end respectively of its own eight-bit code, for a total of 10 or 11 transmitted bits per character. The start/stop bits are there precisely because of the uncertain arrival time of each character. The start bit effectively says "here comes a character," while the stop bit ensures adequate minimum delay between characters. The time duration of each bit that forms a character is constant for any given transmission rate, but the time interval between characters is random (Fig. 6.2).

An advantage of asynchronous communications is that relatively little circuitry is required to handle it. The device that must be attached to a central computer to receive asynchronous communications often costs only $300-$600. However, the usual maximum rate* for asynchronous transmission over telephone lines (see below) is 2000 bits per second (b/s) or about 200 characters per second (c/s) — if one start bit and one stop bit, for a total of 10 bits, are used per character.

*We use "rate" here to indicate the total amount of data that can be transmitted from point to point in a unit time. It is dependent on the time we allow for the signal representing each bit. We use the word "rate" and give our rates in bits per second, as opposed to using the archaic term "baud," which is ambiguous but usually the same as b/s at lower data rates.

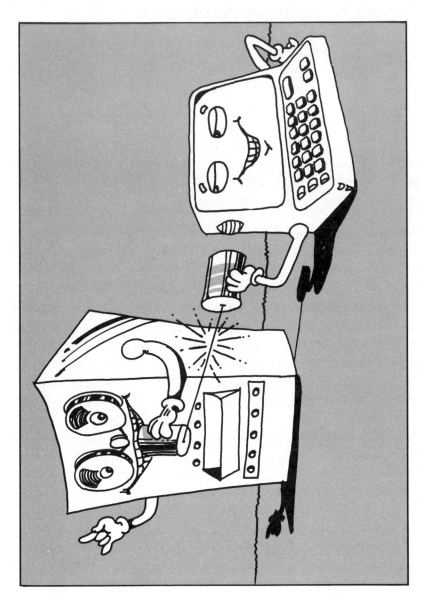

Fig. 6.1. The missing link

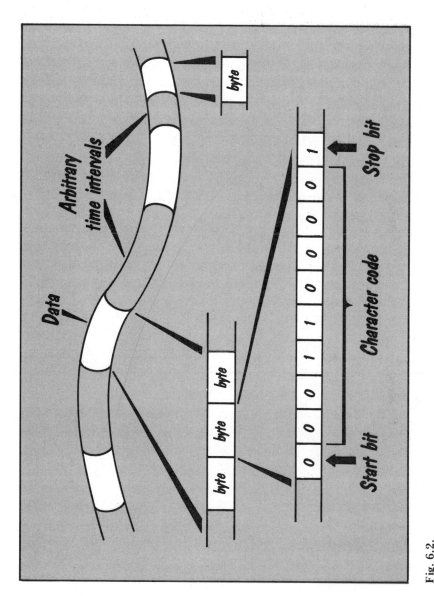

Fig. 6.2.
Asynchronous data transmission (also called "start/stop" transmission).

Asynchronous communications technology is often used in a time-sharing environment in which users at remote terminals send and receive data at relatively low speed. Because asynchronous communication is possible at much higher speed if short runs of wire are used, it is used frequently for high-speed terminals near a computer or for low-speed remote ones.

Synchronous Method

In order to achieve higher data transmission rates and automatic error detection, **synchronous** communications technology is invoked. In synchronous communications, the communications hardware at each end of the linkage is "synchronized" to send or receive data at particular instants in time, and bits of data must be "plugged into" the time slots one after another in lock-step fashion. (See Fig. 6.3.) Complex protocols for synchronous communications exist: Special synchronization characters start a transmission; blocks of characters are sent as a unit instead of one character at a time; "header" characters identify the block of data being sent; and this is all followed by a special block of information used for error checking. Many protocols for synchronous communications have been developed and these will vary from system to system. The potentially higher rate of synchronous transmission and the associated unattended error-detection capability, although necessary to realize the maximum potential from any communications medium, cost more at both the computer and terminal ends. A synchronous communications controller or interface for a single channel usually costs from $3000 to as much as $7000.

Both asynchronous and synchronous communications can operate in either of two modes, which may be dependent on the type of communications hardware you select. These are **full duplex** and **half duplex**.

Full Duplex Mode

Full duplex mode means that the two connected devices are capable of transmitting to or receiving from each other simultaneously. This feature is often exploited by asynchronous communications in a time-sharing environment. Data is transmitted from a terminal to the

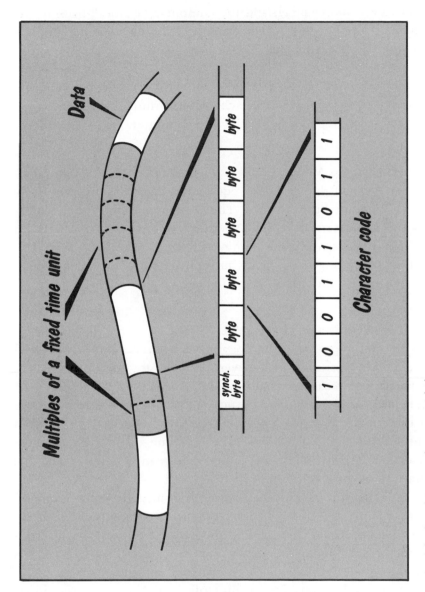

Fig. 6.3. Synchronous data transmission

computer on one channel, and the computer "echoes" back to the terminal on another channel what it received, even while the terminal is sending the next character. Sometimes "send" and "receive" channels operate on different frequencies transmitted on the same wires. Through full duplex operation, you can verify that the computer receives what you send, because the characters printed by your terminal have been received and sent back by the computer.

Half Duplex Mode
In the half duplex mode, equipment can transmit in both directions, but not both at once. The computer cannot immediately echo the characters it receives, because this would interfere with characters being sent by the terminal. Therefore, characters are generated within the terminal, and thus you see only what you type — not what the computer receives.

BRANCHES OF THE FAMILY TREE
Several types of technology have been developed for serial digital communications. Some were created to take advantage of existing communications facilities, and others were the result of research into novel areas. The purpose of the devices is to make the best use possible of communications resources, which may vary from telephone lines to microwaves. The cost and complexity of these devices are commensurate with the performance required and the limitations of the media.

The amount of data that can be transmitted over a communications channel depends upon three things: the strength of the signal; the amount of signal compared to the amount of noise on the channel; and the maximum frequency that the channel can carry. Thus different "grades" of channels are available, and these will be able to carry more or less data in any unit of time. The reader should remember these points during the discussion that follows.

Today, we often wish to locate terminals in offices or areas outside the noise and bustle of the central computer room. For this purpose, cables strung along walls or in the ceiling are quite adequate within a department or building. Plans for today's new buildings should include the installation of such cables and conduits. Such wiring for peripheral devices to a computer is referred to as **hardwired** or *dedicated,* meaning that there is a dedicated cable permanently connecting particular devices.

One encounters difficulty, however, when one seeks to communicate with a computer at some distance. Creating your own hardwired link is expensive and difficult. Fortunately, there already exists a wiring system that goes almost everywhere on this continent and over much of the rest of the world — the telephone system. Some of the most ubiquitous devices for data communications are specifically designed to take advantage of the voice-carrying telephone systems, otherwise known as the direct-distance dialing, or "DDD" network.

The **acoustic coupler** is one device for transmitting digital data over telephone lines. Since the telephone was specifically designed to carry sound (voice), the acoustic coupler translates the sequence of high- and low-voltage levels representing the bits of a character into variations of an audible carrier frequency — for instance, high-frequency for a "one" and low frequency for a "zero." These sounds are piped into the telephone mouthpiece at the sending end by the acoustic coupler; they travel down the line; and they are "listened to" at the receiving end by another coupler that converts the sounds back into voltage levels (bits). To make a good acoustic connection, the headset of an ordinary telephone is pressed into rubber cups in the coupler. Such devices are therefore compatible with ordinary telephones. An acoustic coupler costs as little as $150, although $300–$500 is more typical for a 300 b/s device. The maximum transmission rate for which there exists a commercially available device is 1200 b/s, but such a unit is expensive. The usual transmission rate of these devices is probably adequate for low-speed interactive applications (human–computer dialogue) in which relatively few characters are transacted and low speed is not a limitation.

An attractive aspect of acoustic couplers relates to the mobility they allow. A terminal with such a device can be used anywhere there is a telephone. However, using them on heavily loaded telephone systems, or on a system in which another person can pick up an extension, can lead to frustration with the number of transmission errors encountered.

A device developed along similar lines to make use of the telephone is the **modem** (MOdulator/DEModulator), also called a **dataset.** A modem performs the same function as an acoustic coupler, except that it connects electrically rather than acoustically to the phone line, skipping the step of going through the microphone and speaker in the handset, and thus avoiding distortion. Although the lower end of the speed range of modems overlaps that of acoustic couplers, modems can achieve data rates above 2000 b/s, and even 4800 and 9600 b/s are possible when secure, private lines are used. Above 2000 b/s the synchronous mode is usually used. The cost of higher-speed modems reflects the complex electronics that must be employed in using voice-grade telephone facilities to carry digital communications. For very short distances, though, a less sophisticated, and therefore less costly limited distance dataset (LDDS) can be purchased or obtained from the phone company. The interested reader will find an excellent, more detailed discussion of modem operation in a paper by George M. Dick. [1]

Telephone lines, of course, were developed for carrying human speech, not digital information. The amount of information they can carry in a unit of time is limited. Higher-capacity, more reliable digital communications networks have been established to accommodate the ever-increasing volume of data traffic. In Canada, the DATAPAC service is only one such example. Digital networks are specifically designed to transmit digital data at high frequencies, and therefore the acoustic couplers and modems needed for interfacing with the telephone system are not required. Such digital resources will become more important as time goes on, and we can envision the day when voice communications will take a back seat to more profitable digital data communications.

It would be inefficient to tie up such high-speed lines with one user who might be communicating with a computer at a very low data rate in an interactive mode. Therefore, **multiplexers** are used to collect lower data-rate communications from several users and then to send the combined data from point to point at much higher data rates. At the receiving end, a demultiplexing system separates the data of different users from one another.

For transmission of great quantities of data in short periods of time, high-capacity communications media exist or are under development. Point-to-point ground-based microwave facilities and orbiting satellites are now routinely used by commercial communications carriers to move masses of data at enormous rates. These are especially useful between distant points where lack of direct lines previously necessitated communications over roundabout routes, with all the attendant problems of noise and signal distortion. High-capacity electromagnetic waveguides are hollow tubes that carry data at even greater rates, although their cost limits them to relatively short runs. These latter devices can carry several billion bits per second. At such rates, the entire text of the Bible could be transmitted in about one one-hundredth of a second. [2] Optical fibers using light waves to carry digital signals are under intensive development — a technology of which we shall hear more and more.

Finally, experimentation into the use of the familiar TV cable as a relatively high-capacity carrier of two-way digital information has been under way for several years. If its use becomes economically feasible, our wired society may benefit nicely.

NETWORKS

It is sometimes necessary to develop an organized **network** of data communications pathways in order to link multiple computer systems. There are a number of ways of approaching this problem. Some general cases are shown in Fig. 6.4. Most networks use synchronous communications between points.

The simplest networks are *point-to-point* and *multipoint* networks; each point is called a **node** and is connected at most to only two other points. Multipoint networks string several nodes serially. The drawback of these types of data networks is that a break in the chain isolates some points from each other. For somewhat enhanced reliability, a *ring* network is preferred, since a breakdown at any point in the ring still leaves an alternative pathway for data, back around the loop. Beyond the feature of somewhat enhanced reliability, sim-

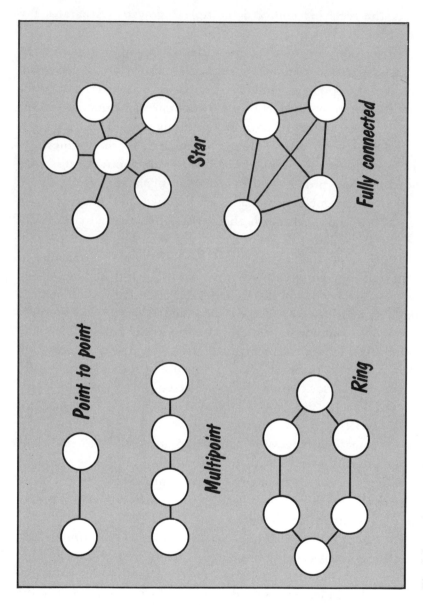

Fig. 6.4. Basic network structures

plicity of routing communications is probably the single greatest motivation for using the ring network approach.

A *star* network connects several peripheral computer systems to a central system. The most complex networks involve links from each point to every other point in the network. Such arrangements, called *fully connected* networks, are the most expensive kinds, because so much equipment is used to interconnect all the nodes.

Although computer networks and **distributed processing** have received a lot of attention recently, so far there has been much more talk than action in this field. It would appear, however, that computer networking is a growing area both within and among institutions.

In considering networks of systems, it must be remembered that even the best communications links cannot help when there are fundamental incompatibilities between different computer systems and their software. A great deal of research is being done to resolve compatibility-related problems and to allow flexible intercommunication of data among systems, especially when multiple database systems are involved.

OTHER COMMUNICATIONS STRUCTURES

Instead of creating a linkage to every remote terminal, a computer can support multiple terminals through **polled** communications. Point of sale (POS) data collection systems — increasingly seen in retail stores — often operate in this manner. The day's transactions are saved in each cash register, possibly on a cassette tape drive. At night, when telephone rates are cheaper, a central computer polls (requests the day's transactions from) each data terminal, one terminal at a time. It does this usually by automatically dialing a telephone to which the terminal is attached, but sometimes via direct wiring with all terminals on the same wire. In the business environment, such a system can be easily used when data must be collected from several locations, but can be sent for central processing later. The advantage of polling is that many terminals can be connected to the same data communications channel without mutual interference, since the main computer permits only one terminal at a time to send data.

This is a good point to define **remote job entry (RJE)**. By means of RJE technology, high-speed input and output devices (for example, a card reader and a line printer) may be located far from a computer. The RJE station reads the input and temporarily saves it. When a block of input is ready for transmission, the RJE equipment sends it synchronously at a high data rate to the main computer. The main computer processes the program and/or data and similarly saves up the output. When blocks of output are ready, a controller on the computer transmits the information to the RJE station, where the output is produced on the local printer. The communications line is used for a minimum time, and when it is used, it is saturated with data at full capacity. Synchronous communication techniques are used, and the data received at either end is checked to detect errors caused by noise or other problems on the line. Formerly, quite expensive controllers were needed in RJE stations, but microprocessor technology is favorably changing this situation.

A FORGOTTEN ALTERNATIVE

There are some applications in which the charges incurred in using long-distance communications links might be considered excessive. Such applications may include either those in which instantaneous communication between points is not necessary, or those in which the volume of data to be transferred is great.

In these circumstances one should not overlook the potential of shipping such storage media as disks or tapes from one place to another. If speed is not important, high-density diskettes holding a million characters of information can be mailed. For large transfers, a courier service may be the answer. Even if it takes two hours to physically carry a three-Megabyte disk cartridge between one computer and another, the effective data transfer rate exceeds 4000 bits per second — better than the usual 2400-bits-per-second rate in most telecommunications networks! When larger-capacity media are involved, the effective transfer rates are even higher. Therefore, as long as the reliability of the messenger can be assured, the taxi, courier or mail services should never be overlooked as potential communications links in computer systems.

TRADE-OFFS

Deciding on the best source for the acquisition of even simple data communications facilities is not necessarily easy. Consider the modem. Some people are aware that this device is readily available from the telephone utility company, but they are probably not aware that the annual rental price for one of these sets can exceed the cost of purchasing one from a modem manufacturer. On the other hand, the telephone company is noted for speedy response when their devices fail: They may replace a defective unit the same day a problem is reported. This **mean time to repair (MTTR)** is hard to beat. It is worth noting, though, that the **mean time between failures (MTBF)** of some modems is reported in terms of 40,000 hours and more. Still another point to consider is that the telephone company will charge you a monthly rental for a **data access arrangement (DAA)**, a device that electrically insulates your external modem from their lines.

Unfortunately, in buying complex high-speed systems the trade-offs among cost, reliability, and service are not easily balanced.

CONCLUSION

An overview as brief and cursory as this cannot provide sufficient background to enable computer system users to fill in, unaided, the "missing links" in their systems. This job is difficult, and may involve significant expenditures that are not always considered in the initial planning of systems. For example, to interconnect three remote computers in a fully connected 2400b/s network requires six modems. If we rented the six modems for $125 a month per unit, it would cost a total of (125 × 6 × 12=) $9000 a year — and we have not yet even considered the cost of synchronous computer interfaces and private telephone lines. Somewhat more economical arrangements might be obtained in some cities, but the overall cost is never negligible.

Even the average computer system consultant is not very knowledgeable in this field. Therefore, the help of communications consultants should be sought when planning anything but the most trivial distributed systems. In Canada, a country well known for communications research, organizations such as the Computer

Communications Network Group at the University of Waterloo and commercial enterprises such as CNCP Telecommunications and Bell Canada have a strong interest in digital communications technology. The help you need is available.

NOTES

1. G. M. Dick, The lowly modem. *Datamation* 23:3:69 (March) 1977.

2. J. Martin, *Telecommunications and the Computer*, Second edition. Englewood Cliffs, N.J.: Prentice-Hall, 1976, p.3.

BIBLIOGRAPHY

Department of Communication, *Branching out: Report of the Canadian Computer/Communications Task Force*, Vols. 1 and 2. Ottawa: 1972.

Edelson, E. I., and L. Pollak, Satellite communications. *Science* 195:1125, 1977.

Farber, D., and P. Barran, The convergence of computing and telecommunications systems. *Science* 195:1166, 1977.

Miller, S. E., Photons in fibers for telecommunication. *Science* 195:1211, 1977.

Modem survey. *Datamation* 25:3:167 (March) 1979.

Stelmach, E. V., *Introduction to Minicomputer Networks*. Maynard, Mass.: Digital Equipment Corporation, 1974.

NEW WORDS

acoustic coupler	mean time to repair (MTTR)
asynchronous	modem
data access arrangement (DAA)	multiplexer
dataset	network
distributed processing	node
full duplex	parallel interface
half duplex	polling
hard-wired	remote job entry (RJE)
mean time between failures (MTBF)	serial interface
	synchronous

7

Skeleton, Monster, or Servant?

Hardware in Summary

Up to this point we have exposed the bare bones of computer hardware. We have separately examined devices that serve various purposes. In reality, none of these devices stand alone. In the same way that all the bones of the body go together to form the skeletal system, individual pieces of hardware combine to form a computer system.

If properly assembled, computer hardware will be a sturdy "skeleton." The addition of appropriate programming can transform the skeleton from lifeless bones into a useful servant that can provide valuable assistance in solving problems in the human environment. (See Fig. 7.1) Improper assembly of the bones can result in a ridiculous hoax — just like the Cardiff "giant" perpetrated by scientific pranksters many years ago. In the worst case, the hapless developer might even create a monster capable of working against its "master." (See Fig. 7.2.)

GOING SHOPPING

Before even considering the problem of acquiring a computer system, you should have studied your environment very carefully, determined those specific problems you want to solve, and come up with what has been called a **functional specification** — that is, a detailed description of what functions the system is to perform and its general characteristics. We suggest enlisting the aid of a computing specialist to do this work. In an ideal situation, you would present this functional specification to potential suppliers who would then indicate what they could or could not tdo for you. At this point, we will skip the important step of writing the functional specification (but temporarily, although most skip it permanently) and deal with it in greater detail in chapter 11.

Here we will instead consider the more common situation today: You find yourself in the position of having to take the responsibility for acquiring a hardware system to meet the specific needs of your office, department, or even your institution. Based on your own functional specification, you are attempting to acquire appropriate equipment from some supplier. We shall discuss the hard-

Fig. 7.1.
Computer hardware can be a sound "skeleton" for a computer system. However, without software it is "lifeless" and useless.

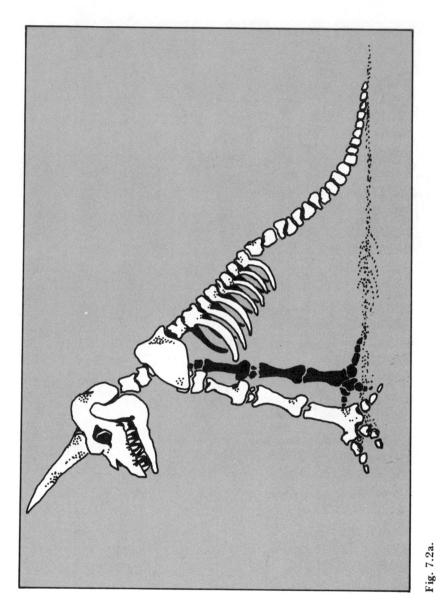

Fig. 7.2a.
Bones are not always assembled correctly. An ancient scholar thought he had discovered a unicorn. The bones really belonged to a mastodon.

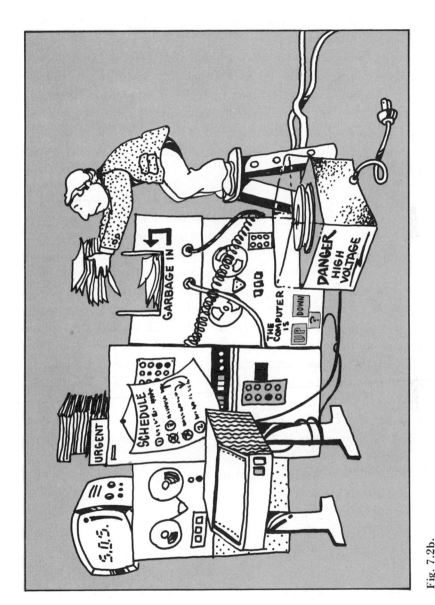

Fig. 7.2b.
Real disservice can be done to an environment by a computer monster. Although all the parts may be there, it doesn't serve a useful function or it demands that everyone scurry around to serve it.

ware part of your total acquisition — temporarily setting aside software considerations.

When listed in detail, the hardware capabilities are known as the **hardware specification**. With this specification in hand, you can "go to the store" to shop for hardware. Selecting equipment is not a small step, since once you actually commit yourself to purchase, you've crossed the Rubicon, and the die is cast.

Your hardware specification will include such items as the following.

1. The kinds of hardware you need: the number and kind of input/output devices, the types and amounts of storage, the type of computer, and the amount of memory and details relating to communications.
2. Detailed requirements relating to each system part in terms of speed, capacity, format (such as tape format), access time, and special features (such as floating-point arithmetic processors).
3. Overall considerations such as the total system **throughput** (the amount of work you intend the system to do in some unit of time), size, power requirements, heat output, availability of and compatibility with software you intend to run on it, and so forth.
4. Company-related considerations: maintenance arrangements, future development, availability of local support, and delivery date.
5. Financial arrangements: purchase, lease or rental cost, discounts, and so forth.

FIRST THINGS FIRST

Under ideal circumstances, you might be able to find a commercially available computer system that meets your hardware specification and gives you the matrix on which to build a system that performs the functions you want. Of course, the sensible customer adjusts performance requirements (to a reasonable extent) so that they are consistent with real products and are not just based on wishful thinking. But suppose no packaged product exists with all the software you need, or at least that none is commercially available as a unit. In this case it would be necessary to hire a system developer (in the form of in-house staff or an external systems house). The system developer would either modify an existing product or create a system from appropriate hardware components (i.e., computer, input/output devices, etc.) and would either write or purchase programs.

Since very few of us know much about writing data processing contracts, we often fail to take adequate precautions at this stage, and we end up bearing inordinate responsibility for the ultimate package. Alternatively, we expect entirely too much of developers — often almost precognition.

The potential user who entrusts system acquisition to outsiders without a contract is performing an act of blind faith. In order to participate intelligently in the writing of a contract, the user must approach the tasks at hand with some understanding of what is involved. In hardware acquisition, much is involved.

BUY, LEASE, RENT

Once you have specified all the parts that make up your system, it will be possible to estimate its cost. When you add up the actual price of all hardware items, you may discover how tentative early rough estimates can be. On the one hand, you may be pleasantly surprised by the ever-falling cost of hardware. More often, your initial enthusiasm over hints of low-cost technology may fade after seeing the final price tag of even a basic microcomputer system. Figures in the ten- to twenty-thousand-dollar range are not uncommon when one requires CRT terminals, hard-copy output, and a useful amount of secondary storage.

Whatever hardware you select, you should obtain a written quotation from each company approached. Such a quotation has a limited period of validity (often 30–90 days), but while it is valid the supplier is committed to supplying the hardware listed at the prices given.

For most micro- and minicomputer systems, the user is typically given only a purchase or lease option, since the availability of a rental arrangement is uncommon when small systems are involved. How you choose to amortize costs depends on the approach of your organization. It should be remembered, however, that a small used computer is worth next to nothing. Today's hardware will be shop-worn and obsolete by the time you are through with it. Furthermore, your used system will probably be unattractive to potential buyers, compared to the hardware then available. Therefore do not count on recouping anything spent on your computer hardware.

There are, nonetheless, companies specializing in the sale of used computers. Sometimes bargains can be had by buying a "cream-puff." If a machine has been maintained under a service contract by the previous owner, you must arrange to continue its maintenance contract under your name. If it has not been maintained, you must try to negotiate preinstallation inspection and adjustment — often an expensive process — if you want to put the equipment on a mainte-nance contract.

When the hardware price is high (as it is especially with larger systems), there may be another way of proceeding: through rental. However, this option may not be open in all situations.

A lease is essentially an arrangement that enables you to bor-row money for the equipment. During the term of a lease (most often five and a half years) the user normally will have the same equipment. But some leases include an agreement to "opt out" on several months' notice, after which you can take out the old equip-ment and bring in the new. This escape clause may require you to pay some penalty for opting out and/or a higher monthly rate. When a lease expires, you usually have three options — you can extend the lease at a greatly reduced monthly rate; you can purchase the equip-ment outright for a lump sum; or you can allow the lease to expire and return the equipment to the lessor. Leasing arrangements for computer hardware usually demand that the lessee (you) buy a main-tenance contract, which typically costs from eight to ten percent of the total hardware price every year.

In approximate figures, on $100,000 worth of hardware, a five-and-a half-year lease would cost the user (66 months × 2.25%) = $148,500. A maintenance contract (assuming a six-month free-warranty period) would cost (8% × $100,000 × 5 years) = $40,000 for a grand total of $188,500 or about $34,273 per year during the lease period.

In a rental agreement, the user pays nothing toward ownership of the hardware; consequently the monthly charge is often substantially lower than in a lease. When the term of a rental agreement expires, the user may either renegotiate or return the equipment to its owner. Unlike a lease, the rental agreement usually includes maintenance. Although it also usually contains an "opt out" clause, there is a financial penalty for terminating a contract prematurely.

Most hardware is manufactured in the United States, and its price is frequently quoted in U.S. dollars, even in foreign countries. However, various taxes and duties substantially increase hardware cost in many countries outside of the United States. In Canada, for example, the buyer would have to pay 20–30 percent more than the list price, and would also suffer the currency exchange difference. Fortunately in Canada at least, many institutions such as hospitals and schools qualify for special exemptions from these extra taxes.

There are alternatives to procuring your own in-house hardware. When the cost is excessive in proportion to the projected use of the machine, it may be best to buy time on someone else's computer — for instance, one owned by a time-sharing service bureau or the lab down the hall.

In some situations, starting a shared facility may be attractive. A group of users might join together to buy a computer (with software that allows sharing) so that they could all use it simultaneously. On the other hand, people who do not need to use a computer all the time might group together to buy a fairly simple machine, and then share it by scheduling its use among themselves.

Choosing a Supplier

If you can afford computer hardware, a number of factors will influence you in the choice of a supplier.

Interestingly, previous contact with a certain kind of machine is a strong influence. Familiarity, instead of breeding contempt, appears to induce a sense of security in computer users. For this reason large computer manufacturers are particularly anxious to have their machines and manuals used in universities. They compete to offer attractive deals to institutions of higher learning because they know that every student is a potential future customer.

Another influence on the consumer is advertising. The general goal is to get your attention through fancy promotion and attractive packaging. [1] Some small computers are deliberately styled to look like their more powerful relatives. Sometimes specifications in hardware advertising may be misleading, though not inaccurate. For instance, a manufacturer might point out that the cycle time of its machine (speed of retrieving an instruction from memory) is 1500 *nanoseconds,* and the unwitting reader may not appreciate that this is the same as all other computers with cycle times of 1.5 *microseconds.* What you really want to know about storage devices is their capacity in bytes (characters), but some manufacturers list their devices' capacities in *bits.* The wary user will divide this figure by the byte length (typically eight) in order to see just how much storage the dealers are talking about. At one time all manufacturers quoted memory storage in words, but now the practice is to quote in bytes. Although the figures are bigger, the memories are the same as before. What you think you see is not necessarily what you get. The wise consumer is hip to the hype.

In all fairness, it must be pointed out that nearly all manufacturers of computer hardware try hard to offer quality products. Their overriding concern, however, is that you should be "sold" on *their* products, for once you have committed yourself to a particular manufacturer, the chances are that you will remain with that one. The only point that should concern you, though, is whether or not a particular product will best suit your specification (both hardware specification and functional specification) for your application. Do not expect the sales representative to relieve you of the final decision; you must make it.

Having distilled the bare facts out of advertising, you may have whittled down the field of competitors to several alternative possibilities that meet your general hardware specifications. It is then necessary to look at the price and performance characteristics of each.

You must first decide whether to take a chance on newly released products or to stick with tried and tested products. The choice could have great bearing on your system's survivability. Obsolescence occurs rapidly in the computer field. Manufacturers may abandon obsolete hardware after a time, leaving users with little potential for upgrading their hardware or sometimes for even obtaining parts or service.

Not only computers but also companies become "obsolete" in this business! This will be true especially in the microcomputer marketplace, where a company can establish itself with little capital, but where fierce competition will drive many new entries into bankruptcy after a short time and thus leave users of those ill-fated systems without support of any kind.

In order to partially insulate their users and themselves against change, some manufacturers build emulators of their previous processors into their newest offerings (or make more advanced systems capable of executing their predecessor's instruction set). In this way users can obtain more modern hardware with better performance than their old hardware, without having to rewrite all their programs. Fortunately, even when a new machine has made obsolete an old and very popular model, a company may continue to market the older computer because of the tremendous user inventory of software for that machine and the company's investment in its own software. Sometimes, though, neither of these things happens.

It is generally advisable to obtain state-of-the-art hardware from a company that has some hope of surviving for several years, unless one plans a project with a short life span and sees no possibility of expansion.

When the need for computer resources will predictably increase over time, some hard decisions must be made because there are at least three initial ways to select hardware. First, you can buy a machine more powerful than initially required, but of course you pay for unused resources until actual usage increases. Second, you can purchase only the machinery you need, making sure that it is capable of future expansion. Finally, you can select an adequate system that is not expandable, but later obtain a separate second system when the need arises. No one approach is always right — users should be aware of all three possibilities and consider which is best for their particular situation.

For larger acquisitions the usual practice is to request tenders (the RFT or Request For Tender) for equipment capable of meeting your specifications. When only a few tens of thousands of dollars are at issue (as for a minicomputer system), it may be to your benefit to create at least an informal competition among several possible suppliers who know that you are "shopping around." Perhaps everyone should consider official tenders.

How long will it take for the hardware you order to be installed on your premises? Sometimes new equipment is shamelessly preannounced. Waiting lists for some new machines are several years long. A manufacturer who supplies a few token machines to an occasional lucky client can technically claim that the product exists. The person who is told to wait 24 months for delivery may feel differently.

Even common peripheral devices may not be as quickly available as one might hope. Usually one must wait at least thirty days after placing an order, and waits of three to six months are common. In this respect, hardware supply houses may help since they stock certain devices. Furthermore, because they buy in volume they can often sell you a particular device at a lower price than the manufacturer will.

The user's preference for one supplier over another should be influenced by the warranty each offers. We have seen warranty periods as short as one month and as long as one year.

When the warranty on your hardware expires, it will be necessary to buy a service contract or to arrange for an in-house group to carry out maintenance (and stock spare parts) since hardware always fails sooner or later. Since the annual cost of a service contract is 8% to 10% of the total hardware purchase price, the advantage of a long warranty period is evident — with a twelve-month free warranty on a $100,000 system you would not have to pay $8000 for maintenance the first year you have the equipment. Maintenance contracts are not all the same. Sometimes there is a "deductible" clause, as in car insurance. The response time to a service call (the time it takes repair personnel to get to your site once you have notified them of a problem) may not be an explicit part of the agreement unless you make sure it is included. How long will it take to obtain spare parts? If long waits are intolerable, will the supplier contract to keep vital spares on site or at least on the company's premises? Beware of buying from suppliers who do not have local offices. Consider these things *before* acquiring any system — not after the hardware you have obtained has been **down** (a genteel term for *kaput*) for a week. Maintenance raises some particularly difficult issues when it comes to decision-making!

In selecting computer hardware one faces a fundamental decision — whether to buy everything from one supplier or to take advantage of the best products of many separate manufacturers. Some companies make peripheral devices that are similar, if not functionally identical, to the offerings of the computer manufacturer. For instance, these devices may be **plug-to-plug compatible**, meaning that they simply plug into the manufacturer's main frame computer without modification. Unfortunately, even plug-to-plug compatible devices are not always compatible with the system software (operating system) of the main computer. Installing such devices may demand modification of the computer's operating system, sometimes by adding software supplied by the peripheral manufacturer. The interchangeable peripheral device market is confusing to the beginner. Consider carefully what you are getting into and if at all possible avoid it completely. If you arc not wary *you* will wind up being the mediator between different companies who blame each other for a given hardware problem. Moreover, *you* get the task of managing warranties, coordinating delivery dates, arranging repairs, and every other job that you could avoid if one company assumed responsibility. Everything has its cost: What you save in money, you can pay for in stomach lining! A much safer approach is to deal with one of the many companies that provide systems made up of diverse components and that also assume full responsibility for all of the hardware.

Some companies manufacture computers designed to imitate better-known machines. For instance, Intel, CDC, and Amdahl all make their own versions of the famous IBM 370. Some minicomputers are capable of imitating those of other manufacturers. Sometimes these machines offer advantages (such as speed) over the original equipment.

When possible, listen carefully to the triumphs and tribulations of other users of similar hardware, but try not to be misled by optimistic or self-serving accounts rendered by those users who want to demonstrate their leadership or sophistication. Remember, there has hardly ever been a computer installation without at least some hardware-related problems.

When the final choice is made, one more factor must be considered. Computer hardware is fragile and it is sometimes damaged during shipment: Insurance should be purchased for transit. Note also that prices quoted for hardware are usually F.O.B. (Freight On Board) at central destinations. If you deal with companies that have no local representative, you may have to pay rather high additional transportation costs.

The Path to Perdition

The actual acquisition of a computer is like "getting religion": It will change your life. However, whether the neophyte progresses or backslides down the path to perdition depends to a degree on attitude.

Some new users welcome their conversion for the wrong reasons. Idolatrous fascination and pride can prevent corrective measures, even in those cases in which a system is patently failing to serve its intended purpose. Even worse off are the sinners who, for financial or political reasons, invest their egos in their hardware. In the kind of atmosphere in which it is not possible to make any decisions except "perfect" ones, critical assessment of a system and its limitations is automatically interpreted as a pesonal attack. It is a classic case of "love me, love my dog." No one can help those who descend through these particular portals.

The Fight Against Extinction

Both of these attitudes are foolish, because the first day of life is also the beginning of the end. The moment computer hardware is acquired, it starts to become obsolete. In some environments many applications of computers are exceptionally mortal. Priorities may seldom remain immutable over a number of years. They may be poorly specified to begin with, and may be altered as true needs are more clearly perceived. Needs sometimes change because of changing technology, altered marketing goals, or fluctuations in the level of financial support. Finally, one may be asking the impossible in demanding radical adaptation in the local environment to suit the introduction of a given system — a fact often discovered only after installation.

Computer hardware, however, is selected to match as closely as possible the needs that have been discerned at one point in time. Foresight may have provided some potential for growth of the system, but inevitably the needs in any environment will change. By the time a computer system is installed, programmed, and functioning it may already be too late: The real world may have passed it by. It is not uncommon for a computer project to fall short of its goals from the first day of operation. Even though a system does initially serve its purpose, change in the environment ensures that the day will come when it will probably be either inadequate or no longer needed. Since a used computer is nearly worthless, this system will probably join the ranks of the many unemployed or semiretired computers.

Newton's Law of Inertia

A given hardware system is somewhat like a photograph of your operation. There is a big financial and emotional commitment in taking the picture, but the picture will have to be updated periodically if the computer is to continue to reflect the current state of affairs and serve as a useful tool. The effort to change an existing computer system — even one that is falling miserably behind current needs — is often painful and expensive. Once you have overcome your own psychological commitment to the status quo, you will have the formidable task of convincing others that change is necessary. At this point many of the nay-sayers who fought most bitterly against the introduction of a computer in the first place may fight just as vigorously against changing the existing computer system. Be prepared for this natural resistance to change. We cannot emphasize too much that rationality and necessity often play a secondary role in the implementation of any computer system.

Computer projects exhibit a great deal of inertia. They are expensive, hard to get used to, and they demand significant adaptation of the organizations that use them. For these reasons, a project that uses computers is difficult to start, hard to redirect, and sometimes nearly impossible to stop, once it is rolling.

Successful "steering" of a computer system is somewhat like flying a huge jet aircraft. [2] It does no good to attempt drastic last-minute alterations in course: The inertia of the craft is so great that it responds only slowly to the controls. To steer your project you must try to anticipate where you want your system to be at a considerable distance in the future, and then apply slow but steady pressure to achieve the necessary course adjustments.

Remember that your computer project is a complex "body" of people and systems. Newton's laws were developed on the model of point masses. It is true that sufficient force will overcome the inertia of any body, resting or moving. However, excessive force exerted over too short a period of time will result in what aircraft designers euphemistically refer to as "hull losses." If you try to start, stop, or redirect a computer project too quickly you will probably destroy it.

BODY WITHOUT SOUL

A paleontologist can assemble the bones of a dinosaur into the appropriate configuration, but nobody can make the skeleton live. Similarly, once you have assembled the bits and pieces of hardware for a computer installation, you still have a lifeless object that does nothing in spite of its high cost and impressive appearance. Do not be deluded by the complex specification and selection process or by the expense of computer hardware into thinking that your problems are over once this machinery sits in your computer room. Your work and financial commitment have just begun. Hardware is a vitally necessary but insufficient part of a computer solution. The right hardware is a step in the right direction. However, even the best hardware is unable to do anything by itself.

System and user programs (software) will be necessary to breathe life into this hardware, and you will have to buy them or hire people to write them. In Part III, therefore, we shall turn our attention to software.

NOTES

1. N. H. McAlister, and H. D. Covvey, Conspicuous computing: or if there are users there must be pushers. *Can. Med. Assoc. J.* 116:183, 1977.

2. D. P. Davies, *Handling the Big Jets,* Third edition. Gloucester, England: Civil Aviation Authority, 1971.

NEW WORDS

down, or downtime

functional specification

hardware specification

plug-to-plug compatible

throughput

PART

SOFTWARE

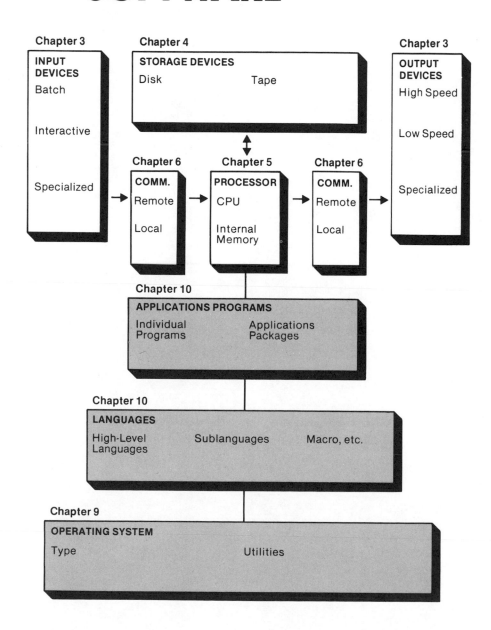

Chapter 3

INPUT DEVICES

Batch

Interactive

Specialized

Chapter 4

STORAGE DEVICES

Disk   Tape

Chapter 3

OUTPUT DEVICES

High Speed

Low Speed

Specialized

Chapter 6

COMM.

Remote

Local

Chapter 5

PROCESSOR

CPU

Internal Memory

Chapter 6

COMM.

Remote

Local

Chapter 10

APPLICATIONS PROGRAMS

Individual Programs   Applications Packages

Chapter 10

LANGUAGES

High-Level Languages   Sublanguages   Macro, etc.

Chapter 9

OPERATING SYSTEM

Type   Utilities

8

How Soft is Software?

The preceding chapters have looked in some detail at computing machinery, or hardware. We have seen that the selection of appropriate hardware for a computer system is not easy.

However, the hard (that is to say, "difficult") part of a computer system is the development of software [1] — the programs that "tell" the computer what to do.

WHAT IS A PROGRAM?

Put most simply, a computer program is a set of instructions in the form of numeric codes that is put into the computer's memory in order to direct its operation. Programming is the art of writing the instructions required to make the computer do what we want it to do.

It should not be surprising that through time programming has evolved as both an art and a science. Computer scientists have improved the methods for formulating, generating, and testing programs, and for insulating themselves from the tedious process of creating the appropriate sequences of numeric codes.

At first, their job was very difficult. Early computers had to be programmed (or coded) through the use of machine language — the actual numeric instructions idiosyncratic to the given machine. Computers can carry out only the most fundamental instructions permitting operations such as "add" or "store." Any particular model of computer is designed to perform a finite number of different instructions (microcomputers generally have a relatively less powerful instruction set than large-scale computers). Because computers are capable of executing only a rather small number of different instructions, it is frequently necessary to combine several instructions in sequence in order to achieve the overall result that we want. For example, to compute the result of the expression A=B+C, the following sequence of machine instructions would be required in most computers.

    clear the accumulator and move B to it
    add C to the accumulator
    move result to A

In other words, the function that we humans expect the computer to perform must be expressed at the machine level by a sequence of steps that is quite microscopic compared to our usual way of thinking.

Machine language, therefore, is only the most rudimentary kind of programming "language." It is very difficult for people to use it. Consequently, over the years computer scientists have created increasingly ingenious translators that convert more human-readable programming languages into machine instructions. Many different programming languages exist today, and each was developed for particular reasons or for a particular type of human program writer. Each is restricted in some regard and is therefore more suited to certain applications than to others.

HARD-WIRED PROGRAMMING

Programming techniques have come a long way since the days of the first computers. The earliest computing machines supported neither programming languages nor programs as we understand them today. The computation to be done was "programmed" by wires that interconnected the various circuits. Each individual circuit could perform some specific function such as "negate" or "increment." The way in which these circuits were wired together determined the overall function performed on the data that was input. In order to provide at least some flexibility, removable electrical panels called **patchboards** permitted the user to "program" at the desk by rearranging the pattern of wires. Obviously, the programming that could be done in this manner was not very powerful, because the physical bulk of the patchboards limited the number of instructions that could be wired by the user. Although such computing was limited to specific kinds of functions, it was sufficient for some early applications in accounting. Historical specimens of these patch-wired machines still exist.

These sorts of computers retained their programs because the programs were implemented in the actual wiring of the machine. Interestingly enough, some recent advances in calculator technology call to mind this early concept. Certain expensive calculators now feature plug-in ROM (read only memory) modules (sometimes called **firmware,** a term for the no-man's land between hardware and software). By plugging in different modules — just as the earliest programmers mounted wired patchboards on their computers — the user can obtain different sets of factory-supplied programs.

THE STORED PROGRAM

Modern computers and the idea of computer programming as we know it developed with the concept of a **stored program** (as opposed to hard-wired programming). In the stored-program concept there is physically no difference between the way program instructions are stored and the way data are stored in the memory of modern computers. This type of machine is often referred to as a "Von Neumann machine." Whether a number in a memory location represents a program instruction or data depends only on how we treat that number. (When a programming error causes the computer to try to execute data as if those data were instructions, the results are unpredictable.)

Historically, entering a program into the computer's memory required significant effort. One of the earliest techniques for entering machine-language programs into the computer's main memory was through the use of dials and switches. For instance, if the (imaginary) instruction for "add" were "1101," then the programmer had to set the front panel switches to "up-up-down-up" and then press another switch to store this in memory. Some programmers became incredibly quick and accurate in programming the machine this way.

Punched cards and punched tape, invented very early in computer history, provided both a convenient way of preparing programs away from the computer and a means of saving machine-language programs for later use. In this case, the numeric instructions were represented by patterns of punched holes instead of by switch or dial positions. The availability of the typewriter-like keyboard devices gave programmers a somewhat more convenient means of entering machine-language programs directly into computers.

Although these latter developments were more convenient than the use of dials or switches, machine-language programming both taxed the patience of programmers and provided them with many opportunities to make errors.

ASSEMBLERS

A new era in programming came with the use of **assemblers.** Each numeric computer instruction was given an alphabetic code, usually of three or more letters. (This short form is also known as a mnemonic code.) For instance, the instruction to add a number to another number stored in an arithmetic register might have been expressed as "ADD." This made life easier for programmers, since it is easier to remember the word "ADD" than to memorize "1101" — the equivalent numeric instruction code.

Assemblers brought another big advantage to programmers. At last they could assign symbolic values to variables. Instead of having to keep track of the actual location of data items in internal memory, a programmer could simply refer to a variable as "A," for example, and let the computer keep track of precisely where that variable was stored. The assembler would accept mnemonic instructions, translate them on a one-to-one basis into the corresponding machine-language instructions, and assign locations for the storage of variables.

Although they are relatively tedious to use, assemblers represent a significant advance over machine-language programming. They use the computer as a tool in the programming process, and thus allow programming to become at least a somewhat more human-compatible activity.

BEYOND ASSEMBLERS

Although infinitely preferable to machine-language programming, assemblers had drawbacks. As we have seen, simple operations such as adding two numbers and saving the result could typically require several instructions. Writing programs to perform more complex **algorithms** (sequences of logical steps to perform specific tasks or operations) was even more complicated. Even the performance of input/output functions is extremely tedious when an assembler language is used. Soon, a "software crisis" of sorts threatened: It was becoming apparent that it was extremely difficult to produce large, reliable pieces of software by using a language as simple as an assembler. Programmers were wasting a lot of time doing the repetitive coding required to implement their designs.

In order to overcome this difficulty, more and more advanced kinds of English-like programming languages have been developed. These languages enable a programmer to express many machine-language instructions in a single statement. An additional advantage of high-level programming languages is that they are nearly machine-independent; this means that a program written for execution on a particular computer can often be executed on a different computer with little modification. Although assembler languages are still used in some places, more programmers these days use a high-level programming language. (FORTRAN and BASIC are but two common high-level languages in widespread use today. A subsequent chapter will deal with programming languages more fully.)

THE PROGRAMMING PROCESS

The encoding of logical steps into some programming language is not particularly difficult. It is the analysis of a problem and the formulation of the logic to be used in solving that problem that are the most difficult aspects of programming. These facts are reflected by different job descriptions for **systems analysts** (those persons who analyze the problem and formulate its solution in the outline of a program) and for **programmers** (those persons who are responsible for encoding the outline into an actual program and testing it). The art of computer programming consists of much more than coding!

The first step is to study the working environment in all its many aspects. Analysts should understand the broad context in which they are working, for it is this environment that gives rise to the problems that need to be addressed by automation. For example, an accounts-receivable program for a doctor's office will be different from accounts-receivable programs for other sorts of businesses. The person or persons doing the programming will need to be familiar with the level of expertise (or lack of it) of the eventual users of the programs, so that they can human-engineer the programs. Only by knowing the individuals for whom a program is being written can one hope to design software that can be used easily and that produces the kind of output desired in an understandable form.

If these studies have been performed properly, the problem or problems to be addressed should emerge clearly in the mind of the analyst/programmer. Possible solutions will then become apparent. Not infrequently, a data processing expert will perceive a possible solution that has nothing to do with automation.

If automation is the appropriate approach, the next step is to organize the solution into a series of logical, step-by-step processes. The logical processes are broken down further into subprocedures and sub-subprocedures, until each small step, in sequence, can be associated with a command or a group of commands in some programming language. Such a process of stepwise refinement is one of the basic principles of **structured programming.**

Many times a programmer will formulate the logic of a program intuitively. Experienced programmers who know their environments will quickly perceive a problem, grasp the solution, and begin to write code, starting at the beginning of a program and working through to its end. Almost subconsciously the good programmer knows what to do. Science-fiction fans will appreciate the analogy to the man from Mars in Heinlein's "Stranger in a Strange Land," who could instantly understand *everything* about something by a mysterious process of comprehensive intuition that he called *"groking."*

Unfortunately, we imperfect earthling programmers are not endowed with this faculty. When we write a program "off the top of our heads," it usually contains mistakes. Either the program will not work at all or it will produce erroneous output. Therefore much additional work normally must be done to correct and verify a program. These processes are called **debugging** and **testing.** These processes are also error-prone, and even when done well do not guarantee the correctness of a program. Even when a program appears to be working, we cannot take its perfection for granted. Some kinds of programming errors (or bugs) can remain hidden throughout many successful executions of a program, only to emerge much later when a particular set of data triggers them and causes their effects to surface.

In addition, once a program has been in use for a while, users may think of extensions or modifications that they would like to see. Their needs may also change over time and thus necessitate revision of a program that had been functioning well up to that point. Therefore, **software maintenance** — the ongoing correction of errors in and modification of working programs — is a late stage of the programming process that never ends.

In an effort to reduce the number of errors that occur in program writing, the science of **software engineering** has provided formal methodologies for the writing and testing of programs. Software engineering will be considered more extensively in a subsequent book in this series. It should be noted in passing, however, that the old technique of **flowcharting** — preparing a logical diagram of the steps involved in a program — is now virtually obsolete. Flowcharting is no substitute for modern program *design* and *testing* methods.

WHEN TO PROGRAM

Creating a computer program and making sure that it works is a difficult job: It requires considerable time and effort by skilled people. Not surprisingly, these skills cost money. The most junior programmer earns at least $10,000 and as much as $14,000. A programmer with a university degree in computer science is worth $12,000 to $16,000. A senior computer scientist with a postgraduate degree and a background in systems analysis commands a salary that starts at $18,000 and that increases with seniority and experience. There is competition for the services of these skilled and expensive personnel. One is sometimes tempted, for budgetary reasons, to thrust a novice programmer into the role of systems analyst. There are times when the results are both satisfactory and economical. However, not uncommonly one gets what one pays for — an inferior design that fails to meet the required objectives. Not merely a false sense of economy is at work in cases such as these, but something worse — the potential for wasting money.

Therefore, in today's economic climate the cost of software development frequently exceeds all hardware-related costs in a computer installation. When the problems of ongoing software maintenance are considered, expenditures for software can easily be double those made for hardware acquisition and maintenance. Clearly, then, the effort necessary to create a program is undertaken only under certain circumstances — when the benefits will justify the work and the expense.

Occasionally a computer program is written to perform one single calculation or one specific set of data manipulations that might take literally years to do in any other way. In such cases the computer program may be used only once, but the effort is essential for lack of a feasible alternative.

Usually, though, the tasks that we program computers to perform are not particularly complex or, for that matter, inordinately time-consuming when they are done once. However, when even a relatively simple task must be performed many times — perhaps each time on different data — then it is beneficial to write a general program that can process *any* legitimate data. The effort required to create the program is reimbursed as the computer repeatedly performs the tasks that cumulatively would have required a lot of human time.

Most business computing applications fall into this latter category. Tasks such as statistical calculations or creation of reports are all carried out quite satisfactorily in most institutions without any computer support. However, when computers are programmed to perform these functions, they soon repay the programming effort by greatly reducing the workload on human beings who previously bore the entire burden of doing this repetitious work.

Of course, when a task is both complex and recurrent, the incentive for writing a computer program is even greater.

NOT SO SOFT

Software is difficult to create, and because of the large amount of effort that must be expended, writing a program is justified only in particular circumstances.

Once it has been created, software can be anything but "soft." On the contrary, it can be completely rigid — that is to say, inflexible. For this reason, the people who create computer programs must often balance the advantages of general-purpose programming against the disadvantages of the added time and cost that are involved. On the other hand, a program directed specifically to one particular type of application may be small and relatively inexpensive to develop. But if it fails to anticipate slightly different needs that may emerge later, the original economy may be wiped out by the need for extensive modifications. Programmers must therefore weigh the pros and cons of more general-purpose programs versus severely specialized programs.

Although research is continually attempting to formalize and "fail-safe" the programming process, the self-programming computer of science fiction does not exist. It is therefore apparent that wherever computers are used, hardware alone is worthless. It is self-deceptive to budget only for hardware-related expenses in a computing project. Software and the people who create it are indispensable components in the development, implementation, and continuing modification of any computer system. In order to achieve anything worthwhile in computing, be prepared to spend the greatest proportion of your investment on software. In other words, put your money where your *people* are!

NOTE

1. M. I. Bernstein, Hardware is easy; it's the software that's hard. *Datamation* 24:2:32 (February) 1978.

NEW WORDS

algorithm

assembler

debugging

firmware

flowcharting

patchboards

programmer

software engineering

software maintenance

stored program

structured programming

systems analyst

testing

9
Bringing Hardware to Life

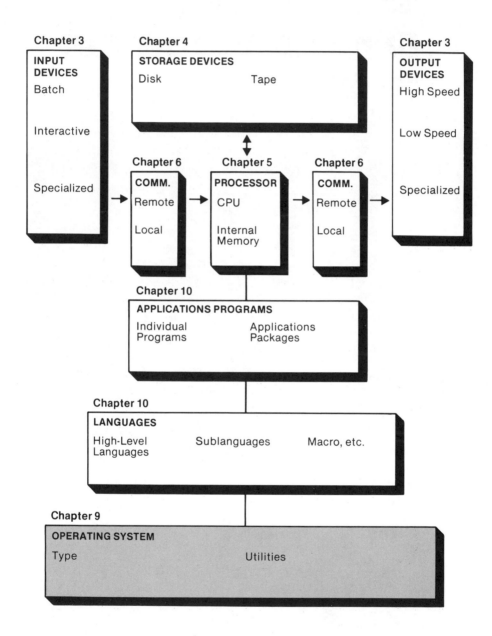

Operating Systems

It is software (programs) that brings computer machinery to life. If hardware is the body of a computer system, software is its soul.

There are two major categories of software: systems programs and applications programs. When specific programs are written to carry out specific users' tasks, these programs are called applications software or applications programs, usually referred to simply as "programs." In the next chapter we will talk about some of the most general features of applications software and the programming languages in which they are written. In this chapter we will discuss one type of systems program — the **operating system.**

The operating system is a level of programming that users do not supply but that has critical impact on the performance of a system for all its users. The operating system — the "master" or "boss" program — controls all the resources of a computer system. The features and limitations of an operating system have an overwhelming influence on the capabilities of a computer system. Therefore, the person responsible for approving decisions to obtain computers must be aware of a few basics.

The more one studies operating systems, the more one becomes aware that no clear-cut divisions really exist. However, for the purposes of basic understanding, it is useful to divide operating systems into somewhat artificial categories: **batch, multistream batch, time-sharing,** and **real-time** operating systems.

A MEANS OF SHARING

When a computer is dedicated to one specific task (job) it may have to do only one thing at a time, one step at a time. Such a computer can wait for the **resources** required to do the job (such as input and output devices, memory, etc.) if they are busy. For such dedicated applications, a simple operating system is all that is needed; its primary function is to provide a standard method of accessing resources.

However, when several users make demands on a system's resources simultaneously, a more complex operating system must exist to permit shared access to resources and to settle conflicts. For instance, when two users request data from a disk at the same time, there must be an operating system capable of giving one user the go-ahead while making the other wait until the first user is finished. This more sophisticated type of operating system is responsible for arbitrating who gets to be first.

There are several reasons why a group of users may share the same computer system. Sharing may be the only way users can afford a computer. An individual, for instance, might not be able to afford a private computer capable of billing. However, it is conceivable that a group of users could economically share the cost of a computer system to handle such needs. A shared system is an advantage when it is not economically feasible for each user to proceed independently.

Although sharing may be dictated by financial considerations, it can also be a virtue, to some extent. When several users share a system, they can also share data, programs, and ideas. This cooperation is especially valuable in an interdependent research environment. A group of users may also be able to afford sharing the sophisticated resources of a machine more powerful than any one of them could afford alone.

Yet if users are to share a system, they must be willing to tolerate some degree of inconvenience. The best operating systems try to minimize this inconvenience while sharing limited resources among all users equitably.

In the simplest case users can take turns, one after the other, in using a computer. This approach is called **scheduled access**. The users themselves do the scheduling. This solution is attractive because it is simple and inexpensive. For a small number of users it may be quite adequate. The operating system for such a machine will be a basic, simple one, because all of the machine's resources will be dedicated to the particular user scheduled to use the computer.

At the next level of complexity, the operating system schedules access to the machine. In a **batch** operating system, many users submit their jobs to the computer at once — often in the form of decks (batches) of punched cards — and the computer then proceeds to execute these jobs as quickly as possible, one after the other. It does this usually by reading in the cards for the first job and doing what they say, then reading in the next batch of cards, and so on. (See Fig. 9.1a.) By taking care of the scheduling, the computer minimizes the time between jobs.

Such simple **batch processing** has its limitations. When a system is designed to deal with only one job at a time, its throughput (number of jobs performed per unit time) is very low. The amount of work that the computer does will be small compared to the potential of the machine. Processors are so fast that, when dedicated to one job (assuming the job is not solving a complex numerical problem — a problem rather rare in reality), they spend very little time actually computing. The CPU is usually idle, waiting for slow operations such as input and output to be completed. When a dedicated processor must wait for input from a terminal, the CPU is wasting time — literally doing nothing. (Remember: a user inputting data may average one character/second; a computer could execute a million instructions during a second.) In single-task computers, the percentage of **processor utilization** (the amount of time the computer spends actually executing instructions divided by the total elapsed time X 100) may be very low.

One solution to this efficiency problem is the **multistream batch** system (Fig. 9.1b) which allows multiple jobs (batches) to run apparently simultaneously by giving another job a resource as soon as a previous job is through with it. Thus one job can be using the CPU, another the disk, etc. The resources are kept busy and for all practical purposes several jobs are getting done at once.

TIME-DRIVEN OPERATING SYSTEMS

There are several ways in which an operating system can be designed to make use of what would otherwise be idle CPU time in order to accommodate multiple users. In a **time-sharing** operating system the computer's central processing unit devotes a finite amount of time (a time slice) to each user's program in sequence.

There are two kinds of time-sharing. The oldest and least efficient is called **swapping**. When job A's turn (time slice) has expired, it is transferred out of main memory onto secondary storage (disk). Job B is then read from disk into main memory, executed for a time,

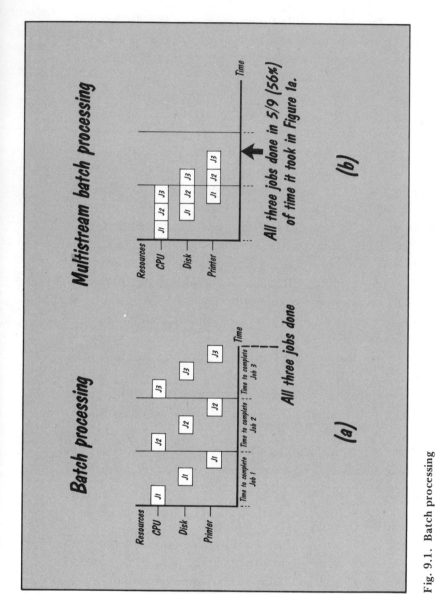

Fig. 9.1. Batch processing

(a) In a batch processing system, a job (a batch of cards or the equivalent) is processed completely, then the next job, and so on. Each job uses whatever system resource it needs, when needed. Between the times a resource is used, the resource is idle — wasted. This idle time could be used if a proper method of assigning resources to other jobs (i.e., sharing the resources) were available. (b) One such way of sharing is to have several jobs waiting in line and to assign a given resource to one of them when a previous job has released the resource. This will use the wasted time and it will appear that several jobs are being done at the same time. Such a system is called a multistream batch system.

and then put back onto disk, so that the computer can turn its attention to job C. When job A's turn comes round again, it is read back into main memory and execution is resumed. The process repeats indefinitely in a "round robin" fashion until each job is completed. (See Fig. 9.2.) The disadvantage of swapping is that a significant portion of the computer's time is spent in switching from job to job (taking programs and data to and from disk) — a process during which no actual execution of the users' instructions is carried out.

A modern method of time-sharing is one in which all the jobs to be time-shared remain resident in internal memory until they are completed — whether or not they are actively being executed. With the decreasing cost of memory, this has become the more common method. In many modern systems swapping is a recourse only when main memory is full. In the memory-resident case, the operating system executes each user's instructions for a short time, then goes to the next user, and so on, but the step of moving each user's program to and from disk is eliminated. There is still some time wasted in switching from job to job but this is very much reduced compared to the swapping approach.

Time-sharing works amazingly well in certain applications. The fact that the computer can easily cope with the (for it) light workload of apparently doing several jobs simultaneously gives each person the illusion of sole use of the machine. The computer can serve many users, making its use feasible where it would otherwise be economically impractical.

Sharing extends to resources other than the processor — such as disk. However, the utilization of other resources is sequential, on a first-come-first-served basis. For example, when you need data or have some data ready to be saved or printed, your request for the disk or printer is **queued** and you will be given service as soon as your turn comes up.

The ultimate basis for time-sharing is the assumption that users do relatively little computing (use of the CPU), and that the system quickly gets to the point of waiting for user input or for slow output terminals to type out results. During this I/O time other users can be served. It is easy to see ultimate, practical limits on any system, however, since sooner or later the waiting periods in queues for various

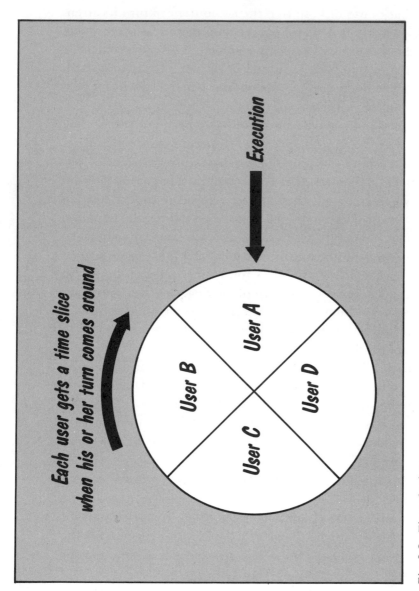

Fig. 9.2. Time-sharing
The central processing unit (CPU) is dedicated to each job (user program) for a short period of time. Even though only milliseconds are involved, the CPU can execute thousands of instructions during each time slice. The round robin "rotates" on the order of a hundred times per second. The general idea here is that a job should be complete in a very few "rotations." If not, then the overhead (the time taken to switch from job to job — ignored in the diagram) is excessive. Special (algorithmic) procedures exist in some systems to give a larger time slice to jobs that remain in the round robin too long. Thus the jobs are finished off, and overhead is reduced.

resources will become lengthy, and the system will simply take too long to complete any one job. An interesting point to note is that a very powerful processor will not help here; access to other slower resources is the "rate limiting step." A system limited by the length of (actually, the time spent in) I/O queues is called **I/O bound.**

EVENT-DRIVEN OPERATING SYSTEMS

There is a class of circumstances for which time-sharing operating systems are not suitable. If, for instance, we must detect an event or measure it in real time (that is, as it happens), the computer obviously must act when the event occurs — not when the computer chooses to do so. An operating system that can respond to events as they happen is **event-driven** and is called a **real-time** operating system. A real-time operating system allows external devices to preempt the computer's attention precisely when they need it. Even time itself can be used to drive the system; in this case an electronic signal occurring at a given rate (called a **real-time clock**) is the "event" to which the system responds.

Real-time operating systems come in simple and complex varieties. An event-driven system dedicated to a single task (job) simply waits for events to occur and then does what it is supposed to do (such as perform a measurement or a computation). A **multitasking** or **multiprogramming** system is one that attempts to cope with several tasks at the same time by interspersing their component computational parts and by scheduling access to system resources. In this case, requests for resources must be coordinated because they are driven by external happenings in the real world. Sooner or later conflicts will occur between jobs contending for the same resource at the same time. At this point, the only solution is to allocate resources according to some predefined priority, favoring one task while sacrificing others. The favored job is served immediately, but lower-priority tasks will not get that resource until the other job has finished with it. It is up to the system designer to ensure that conflicts are resolved quickly enough and that even if there are delays, the system in general "keeps up." (See Fig. 9.3.)

Ideally, a real-time operating system would inform users when conflicts occur or would at least be able to generate output indi-

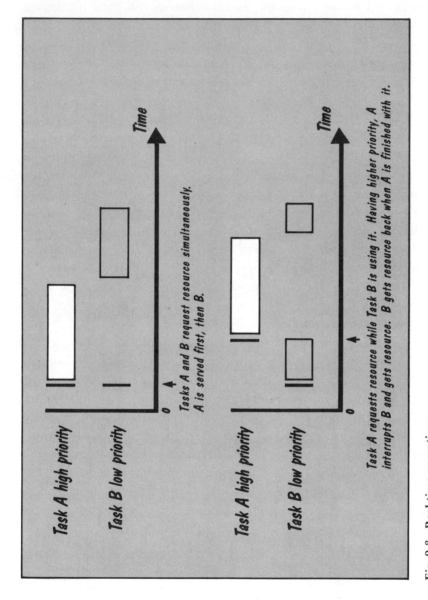

Fig. 9.3. Real-time operation

cating how conflicts had been resolved. In practice, this kind of service is rare.

Many other ingenious operating systems have been designed in an effort to give the greatest number of users the best possible service in a multitasking system. Some operating systems are hybrids, combining features of both time-driven and event-driven systems. A certain number of jobs are time-shared in what we will call the **background**. These background jobs have low priority and can be preempted at any time by a job running in the **foreground**. In other words, the foreground job has top-priority access to resources.

Some operating systems have the ability to juggle the way in which they allocate resources to optimize overall system responsiveness. They have special programs that are able to discern what is happening and to adjust scheduling of resources to needs. They differ from other operating systems in their adaptability to different demands placed on them.

LIMITATIONS

Many multitasking operating systems theoretically permit a large number of jobs to be done apparently at the same time. In practice, however, the whole process breaks down at some point in every system. For one thing, it takes time (called **overhead**), to switch from the job currently being executed to another. A certain amount of time is lost from every second. If a computer is asked to perform too many tasks or to serve too many users, at some point it will just not get around to completing a given assignment in time or at least sufficiently quickly to satisfy a user. Some time-shared operating systems are sufficiently advanced so that when they perceive one job coming around for execution too many times (and thus generating unacceptable overhead by taking too long to finish) they will give that job a large time slice in order to finish it off and get it out of the way.

OTHER FUNCTIONS OF OPERATING SYSTEMS

Besides permitting sharing of resources, a useful operating system will provide other services essential to the operation of a shared computer system. Not all operating systems provide every one of these features, but the better ones will provide most of them.

The operating system *protects* individual users and their data from one another and from intruders. It controls access to the system by passwords, ensures that users' programs do not interfere with each other during execution, and makes certain that users cannot tamper with each other's data either accidentally or maliciously.

An operating system will provide resources to permit **backup** — the copying of all data and programs contained on the system's disks onto other disks or less accident-prone media such as magnetic tape. **Transaction logging,** a process that keeps a copy (usually on magnetic tape) of every user interaction with the computer, may also be provided.

The operating system is also responsible for doing *accounting* of system utilization, especially in commercial installations that sell computer time.

If desired, the operating system can provide *statistics* on resource utilization so that adjustments to its methods of allocating these resources can be made as required.

Finally, the operating system provides all users with standard methods of *storing, retrieving,* and *transferring data* — even between jobs when necessary. It can also provide **device independence**; this means that users need not be aware of the precise characteristics of the devices that are used for input, output, and storage.

PROBLEMS WITH OPERATING SYSTEMS

Operating systems are among the most intricate programs ever devised; for some of them, development time was in thousands of man-years — person-years today! [1] Because these programs are so complex, it is just about impossible to get all the **bugs** (or errors) out of them. These programs can be executed in a nearly infinite number of ways, with the result that perfection is impossible. Every run is a test. Users therefore will note problems from time to time and report them to the company that supplied the system. This company will provide corrections (**patches**) and will periodically reissue a revised version of the operating system. New versions of an operating system are usually palliative measures designed to squash old bugs — but sometimes they introduce new ones of their own.

The never-ending campaign against bugs necessitates the purchase of a **software maintenance contract** by the user, so that the old operating system will be replaced by "refined" versions as they become available. Updates may occur up to several times a year. An operating system is expensive, and in the case of purchased operating systems, yearly software maintenance costs the user up to one-third of the original cost of the software.

Not only do operating systems contain errors, but they may also on occasion be the limiting features in system expansion. For example, it may be impossible to add more disk storage to a computer simply because the operating system was not designed to handle that much secondary memory.

A couple of final observations should be made regarding the limitations imposed by operating systems. Generally, the more complex the system, the more memory it will require. Advanced operating systems for big machines can occupy large amounts of internal memory. Internal memory used by an operating system is usually not available for user programs. If a system is tailored for a specific application, its operating system will probably be reasonably small — but if the operating system is designed for a general-purpose system, it will be correspondingly larger.

Another restriction of operating systems is that in general, the bigger they are, the longer they take to perform their functions. Users who demand a sophisticated operating system may find system performance slowed down in direct proportion to their demands for sophistication.

DOING THE IMPOSSIBLE

We make nearly impossible demands on operating systems. Time-shared operating systems are supposed to facilitate sharing of computer resources among many users, but they must achieve this sharing in such a way that any individual user thinks that he or she has sole use of the computer. What is worse, operating systems are forced to do this "on the fly" because the demands on them are unknown until after those demands are actually made.

In a computer installation designed to serve more than one user at a time — as is the case even with the majority of minicomputers today — the operating system is a vital consideration. If the right one is chosen, it will seem to do the impossible, but an inappropriate one will be a source of continuing frustration and perhaps ultimately of project failure. Therefore, before you get involved with any computer, carefully choose and get to know its operating systems. The operating system is the software that gives "life" to inanimate hardware. In many ways it is the operating system that gives a computer its characteristic "personality" — a fact that is nowhere as obvious as in those cases in which several companies supply different operating systems for the same hardware. The resulting systems can be radically different in what they can do and in the types of applications they can serve.

NOTE

1. F. P. Brooks, *The Mythical Man-month: Essays on Software Engineering.* Reading, Mass.: Addison-Wesley, 1975.

BIBLIOGRAPHY

Hansen, P. B., *Operating System Principles.* Englewood Cliffs, N.J.: Prentice-Hall, 1973.

Lister, A. M., *Fundamentals of Operating Systems.* London, England: Macmillan, 1975.

NEW WORDS

background

backup

batch operating system

batch processing

bug

device independence

event-driven

foreground

I/O bound

multiprogramming

multistream batch operating system

multitasking

operating system

overhead

patch

processor utilization

queue

real-time clock

real-time operating system

resources   task

scheduled access   time-sharing

software maintenance contract   time-sharing operating system

swapping   transaction logging

10

The Dawn of Language

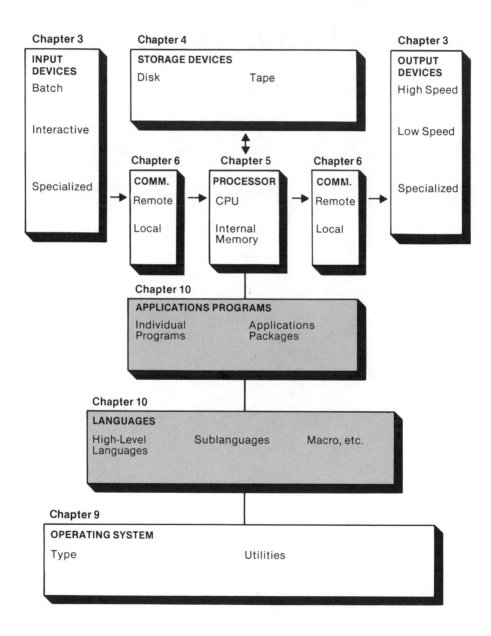

Programming Languages and Applications Packages

In Chapter 8 we saw that computers are able to "understand" only instructions coded in machine language — the numeric codes that instruct the machine to perform its most basic, primitive functions. Machine language is difficult for people to comprehend. Consequently, computer scientists have created system software that converts applications programs written in more human-readable programming languages into the machine-language instructions that computers can carry out. There are numerous different programming languages, each developed for particular kinds of applications. Each language has individual strengths and weaknesses, depending on the purposes for which it was created.

Some programming languages are function-related — that is, they have been developed to cope with a general area of data processing such as database management or scientific calculation. Other languages have been created to serve specific target areas such as medicine, business, or scientific programming.

No one programming language is ideal in all circumstances. Therefore, the evaluation of a given computer system includes consideration of the programming language(s) available on that system. In an **in-house** operation, the languages used may affect the productivity of your programmers and the kinds of programs that they can write for you. For example, a language designed to facilitate arithmetic calculations may be awkward for character-string (text) manipulation. Even in a packaged computer instrument bought from a supplier, the language that the developer used in writing the program is important, since it may affect the ease with which you or your supplier can modify such a system in the future. Finally, whatever programs you do acquire for whatever applications, they will be written in some language: The computer system you use must support that language.

The purpose of this chapter is to give the reader an overview of the general sorts of programming languages available for different kinds of programming applications. It is not our intention here to provide an exhaustive list of all programming languages or to give detailed instructions on how to program in any particular language. Computer programming is a profession that normally lies far outside the interest or skills of the average person. Those who do wish to study the techniques of programming and the syntactic and semantic differences among various programming languages may seek this information in computer science textbooks, such as Nicholls' *The Structure and Design of Programming Languages* (Addison-Wesley, 1975).

TAKING SHORTCUTS: THE MACRO ASSEMBLER

In Chapter 8 we saw that assembler languages translate mnemonic, alphabetic codes into machine-language instructions on a one-to-one basis. Although this was an improvement over machine-language programming, it was still fairly tedious.

The next enhancement of assembler programming languages was to allow programmers to save on some secondary storage medium the **routines** (short parts of a program or a related series of program instructions) that they frequently used. Programmers could associate a new mnemonic — called a **macro** — with each routine, and these routines could thereafter be replaced in programs by macro instructions. Every time the assembler saw one of these macros, it would automatically substitute the appropriate series of assembler instructions. A library of useful macros enabled an assembler programmer to be more productive because it eliminated much repetitious coding.

Sophisticated macro assemblers are still very much in use. Assembler language programming is generally used when programmers need to manipulate the individual locations or the bits of computer memory. Most operating systems (which are themselves programs) are written in assembler.

An assembler can be a powerful, efficient tool to produce the fastest kinds of programs that use the least memory — a fact that may be important in certain real-time applications, especially in support of instrumentation. However, assembler language programming is tricky. Assembler programs are often lengthy, and errors in them may be difficult to find or to prevent. Programmers who must modify an assembler language program that they did not themselves write may have a difficult time in simply trying to figure out how the program works before they can even consider modifying it. In fact, assembler language software is obscure enough that companies can usually count on its acting as a form of encryption, effectively protecting their proprietary software from modification by outsiders.

Computer applications are not static, and ultimately one must face updating the applications software. Sometimes companies can be trusted to do this, sometimes at a reasonable cost. If not, then updating will fall to in-house staff. The use of assembler language programming may therefore be an especially critical problem in some environments.

HIGHER-LEVEL LANGUAGES

Assembler languages are closer to machine instructions than to human language. Since developers recognized this handicap affecting human productivity, they saw the need for programming languages closer to our way of expressing logical procedures, arithmetic calculations, and textual manipulations. Today there are many higher-level programming languages: ALGOL, BASIC, COBOL, FORTRAN, PASCAL, RPG, and SNOBOL, to name but a few of a very long list. Their variety attests to the diverse purposes for which they were created. These languages are not as high-level as everyday human language. They still require trained programmers to use them effectively, although an introduction to any one of the programming languages is sufficient to get a neophyte started.

Compilers

Getting closer to the human way of expressing problems demands that the computer do more work for us. A compiler takes source code written in a higher-level language and translates it into **object code**. Object code may be machine language, directly executable by the computer, or it may be an intermediate language that requires another translation step at execution time to get to machine

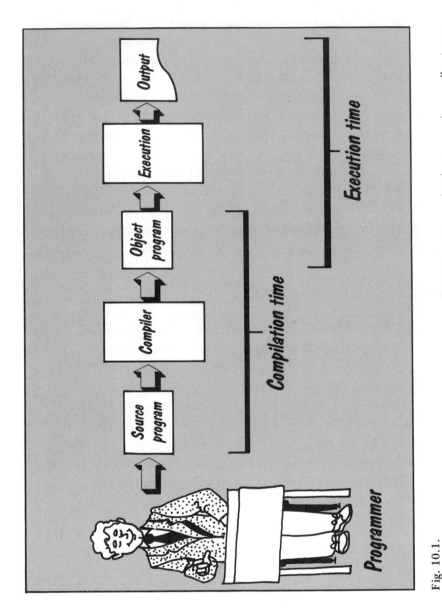

Fig. 10.1.
A programmer writes a *source program* in a human-readable programming language. A compiler translates these English-like statements into instructions that the computer can execute – an *object program*. At execution, the computer usually does further processing of the object program (adding library routines, etc.), and then the program is executed and its *output* is produced.

language. A translation process much more complex than the simple one-to-one translation characteristic of the assembler is used. This allows the closer-to-the-human form of expression. (See Fig. 10.1.)

One of the earlier but most durable languages using a compiler is FORTRAN, an acronym that stands for FORmula TRANslator. As the name suggests, this language was designed for scientists. It permits them to say, for instance, "C=(A+B)*3.125/E" close to the way we would write it algebraically: "C=(A+B) $\times$ 3.125$\div$E" — an expression that would require many machine-language or assembler instructions to program.

Other languages were developed for different purposes. COBOL is a business language. Although some consider it cumbersome and verbose, it is nevertheless fairly easy to learn, permits flexible manipulation of text strings and the handling of data files on secondary storage, and supports the inclusion of nonexecutable comments to assist others in understanding the programs. Still another language is ALGOL — a language that seems to be preferred by people involved in numerical analysis.

There are many other compiled languages, and each can support some kinds of applications more easily than others.

A certain degree of **software transportability** — the ability to take a program written on one computer and run it on a different computer — has been realized through the use of high-level languages. They depend on a "standard" human-readable language and not on the machine language of individual computer models. Adherence to these standards is, however, not universal. FORTRAN, for example, has undergone numerous revisions during the past decade, and every company seems to have its own variations, incompatible with those of other companies. Each nonstandard extension of a common language gives added flexibility to programming, but it also has the negative effect of closely binding a user to one company or even to one machine type. Often an institution will use the machines of only one manufacturer, with the hope that programs can be run on all computers in that institution without modification. This can be a vain hope, however, since the same manufacturer may change its versions of programming languages from model to model or even between different releases of the same operating system.

Some compilers are smarter than others. Some are **optimizing compilers** that automatically correct obvious inefficiencies in source programming. As one might expect, faster compilers with more luxury features are usually available on larger computers. Today they can sometimes be found even on minicomputers.

New languages are constantly being developed and released for use. Not many of these ever seem to achieve widespread popularity. Instead, programmers seem to prefer a few long-established programming languages [1] — possibly because of previous training and simple familiarity.

Interpreters

Another approach to the implementation of a high-level programming language is the interpreter. Interpreters do not produce machine-language object code for a whole program (as in the case of compilers). Instead, they accept source language and interpret it one small segment at a time, executing the user program piece by piece as each portion is encountered. When the interpreter moves on to the next part of the code, it "forgets" the previous part it has just executed. A large amount of overhead is involved in processing with an interpreter. Instead of compiling a source program only once and then executing machine language thereafter, each little piece of source code has to be translated every single time it is encountered, before it can be executed.

BASIC (a simplified FORTRAN-like language), is probably the most widespread interpretive high-level language. BASIC is a common language for the so-called "personal" microcomputers. Other languages such as APL (a language favored by mathematicians) are also popular interpreters. In the medical environment, MUMPS is a well-known interpreter for database manipulations. (It is really a language implemented as part of an operating system.) LISP is an interpreter used mostly by artificial-intelligence researchers.

Although interpreters are slow compared to compilers, they offer some advantages. When a user wants to **debug** (correct) a program, an interpreter can make the job easier since the source code is always available at any point in execution. A program can be stopped and changed, and its execution can be resumed far more easily than with most compilers. Therefore, occasionally a popular language will be available in both interpretive and compiler mode — the former for debugging, the latter for high-speed execution after the bugs have been corrected.

In this discussion we have (for the sake of simplicity) deliberately avoided some of the more detailed technical aspects of the area such as overlaying techniques, different structures of languages, and compiler and interpreter design. Interested readers can refer to many textbooks in a computer science library on the topics of languages and compilers.

Beyond High-Level Languages

The ultimate goal in the quest for a human-like programming language would be a computer that could understand ordinary (or "natural") language and formulate its own program. Of course, only very limited examples of such ideals exist, although one of the Holy Grails of artificial-intelligence research is to develop such a language.

However, computer scientists are continuously striving to develop programming languages that are less and less dependent on exact syntax. Less formal languages would enable nonprogrammers to instruct computers to perform certain tasks. Some success in this area has been realized with **query languages** — languages that allow a person to sit down at a terminal and request from a database the data that meet the criteria specified. The ultimate goal here is that users should be able to instruct the computer *what* they want done in as normal a way as possible — they should not have to tell it *how* they want it done, as required by most of today's languages.

Extensions to High-Level Languages

For specialized applications, an ordinary programming language may not have all the required features. For this reason, various sublanguages that append to a regular high-level language have been written. A **data management language** (DML) is a special sublanguage for handling data storage and retrieval in a database system. A **data definition language** (DDL) enables one to structure (organize) the storage of data on secondary-storage devices. Real-time systems must include appropriate extensions to their programming languages for such applications as analog-to-digital conversion.

APPLICATIONS PROGRAMS AND PACKAGES

We usually label as "programs" those sets of instructions (written in some programming language) that direct the computer to perform a specific task or operation.

There are certain kinds of programs commonly needed by many users. Statistics is a prime example of an application area important to many. People who use computers in areas such as statistics are not interested in computer programming; they only want the computer to supply results. To serve users like these, various companies market software **applications packages,** designed to be easily implemented by many different users. In statistics, for example, SPSS and BMD are two well-known and proved packages. Detailed instruction manuals enable a computer-naive user who understands statistics to process his or her own data. The usual vehicle for data input in such systems is punched cards. A version of SPSS called SCSS also exists; this adaptation allows users to manipulate their data via a terminal.

There are many other applications packages designed to meet widely different needs. For instance, there are many packages for producing graphs on various kinds of graphics terminals.

There are advantages in using software packages. The cost of purchasing such packages can be much less than your cost of developing them. The reason is that the companies developing sophisticated programs can spread out their costs over hundreds or even thousands of users, each of whom pays relatively small fees to use the final product. Packages are usually well-tested in the field, thanks to scores of users who have employed them in different circumstances. Another advantage is that the use of a common applications package forces users into a common input format, sometimes permitting data-sharing where necessary.

Some companies market specific software packages with specific hardware systems as complete, integrated products. These are called **turnkey systems.** This practice is common in business systems in which hardware is provided along with applications packages to deal with business problems such as payroll, accounts receivable, etc.

The main disadvantage of applications packages is that they are often large and monolithic. You take all or nothing. This may make them unsuitable for small micro- or minicomputer installations. The user who needs only basic statistical analysis may be frustrated when the other seventy statistical tests that are part of a package will not fit into the organization's small computer. Another potential drawback is that some applications packages are copyrighted and cannot normally be modified to suit individual users.

As a rule, the user is well-advised to purchase, lease, or rent a software package if one exists for the kind of application needed. It does not make economic sense to "reinvent the wheel."

THE LANGUAGE HIERARCHY

There has been a steady evolution of programming languages from primitive machine language to the most sophisticated optimizing compilers. The languages at each level have specific uses, and each language in the hierarchy represents a significant advance over lower levels. (See Fig. 10.2.)

The particular needs of certain types of applications have spurred the evolution of new species among high-level languages. These needs can be as diverse as those associated with high-level

Machine language	01101000	00001000	
	01110000	00001001	
	00010100	00001010	
Assembler	CLA	A	
	ADD	B	
	STO	C	
High-level languages	C = A + B		(FORTRAN — a scientific language)
	ADD A TO B GIVING C.		(COBOL — a business language)

Fig. 10.2. The hierarchy of programming languages
Each level represents a step closer to human ways of expressing instructions.

mathematics (needs that spawned APL), or those associated with database management in a medical environment (needs that gave rise to MUMPS). Applications packages have developed in response to similar needs in many environments.

However, different computers may support different programming languages and consequently different software packages. Consideration of these software features, therefore, is essential in setting up any computer application.

In some environments, computing needs are likely to change frequently. A dynamic research situation may necessitate a continuous process of program writing and rewriting. Alternatively, failure to thoroughly study a problem before writing programs will automatically pave the way for software modifications. It makes sense to use a programming language that can be a powerful tool to the original programmers and that can be understood by future programmers who may have to modify programs they did not write. The installation that uses assembler-level programming or some obscure higher-level language not well known to most programmers may have difficulties. It has been shown that programmers generally produce the same number of lines of source code daily, whether they are using low-level assembler language or high-level languages. High-level languages can often accomplish more in one line of code than a dozen or more assembler-language statements could. Economics dictates that a high-level language is preferable, whenever it is possible to use one.

Factors such as the speed of execution, the kind of computer along with the amount of internal memory required to support different languages, and the availability of specific needed language features must all be considered before a system design can be finalized.

The cost of programming languages must also be reckoned in the planning of any system. In any given system, the system software may come either **bundled** (its cost included with the price of the hardware) or **unbundled** (its cost figured separately). Unbundled costs make up a significant proportion of the whole system cost. A BASIC interpreter for a microcomputer system typically costs from $400 to $800. A COBOL compiler for a minicomputer can cost up to $10,000. When several different kinds of applications are contemplated that may require several languages, the cost of providing these languages cannot be ignored. Finally, there is an annual cost associated with their maintenance by the supplier.

It must also be remembered that programming languages are intimately dependent on the operating system of the computer on which they run. The operating system may therefore dictate which languages you can use.

Even an excellent computer system with an appropriate operating system and a superb high-level language may not be appropriate if a needed applications package is not available on that machine, in a language that the machine supports.

CHOOSING YOUR TOOLS

Obviously, then, these are things to think about before acquiring a system. Programming languages and applications packages are the fundamental tools that permit programmers and users to approach the particular job at hand. Select these tools carefully. An artist can use a sharp chisel to work wonders with wood but cannot use a chisel to paint pictures.

NOTE

1. A. S. Philippakis, A popularity contest for languages. *Datamation* 23:12:81 (December) 1977.

NEW WORDS

(applications) package

bundled

data definition language

data management language

debug

in-house

macro

object code

optimizing compiler

query language

routine

software transportability

turnkey system

unbundled

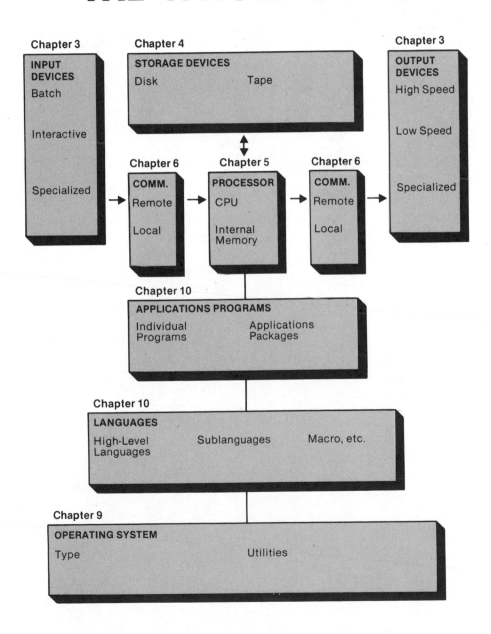

Chapter 3

INPUT DEVICES

Batch

Interactive

Specialized

Chapter 4

STORAGE DEVICES

Disk   Tape

Chapter 3

OUTPUT DEVICES

High Speed

Low Speed

Specialized

Chapter 6

COMM.

Remote

Local

Chapter 5

PROCESSOR

CPU

Internal Memory

Chapter 6

COMM.

Remote

Local

Chapter 10

APPLICATIONS PROGRAMS

Individual Programs   Applications Packages

Chapter 10

LANGUAGES

High-Level Languages   Sublanguages   Macro, etc.

Chapter 9

OPERATING SYSTEM

Type   Utilities

11
The System in Situ

Computer Systems in the Human Environment

Computer hardware and software are the two fundamental components that, when combined, make a computer system. There is, however, one more element essential to the effective application of computers in any environment — people.

People must ultimately use, and are supposed to benefit from, the computer in an operational setting. They should be involved with system-design experts from the very beginning, thereby contributing to the process of specifying and selecting any system. In many situations computer professionals (programmers, analysts, etc.) will be needed to develop software and to modify programs from time to time. If development is going to be carried out in-house, then these individuals will be part of the on-site team. People will be needed to run the computer or at least to change tapes and disks (computer operators), and to collect data and enter this data into the computer (data entry clerks). This will necessitate a redefinition of existing office-staff roles, or in some cases, the hiring of additional staff. Furthermore, if output from the computer is to be used to the best advantage, the staff must be educated in how to use output. Inevitably, there must also be an effort to overcome misconceptions about what the new tool can do. User training is essential so that the tool can become familiar enough to be usable.

It seems appropriate, then, after dealing in such detail with the characteristics of hardware and software, that we consider the computer system *in situ* and focus on the people who put it there, keep it working, and use it.

THE WELL-TEMPERED SYSTEM

A computer system intended to have a reasonable impact on an environment does not magically appear one day. Successful implementation of any computer application is the culmination of a lengthy and thoughtful process [1] involving many individuals.

First among these people are those who perceive the need for, analyze the effects of, and plan the system — systems analysts. To avoid conceiving a fiasco, they must do their homework and proceed in an organized and cautious way to document whatever area they intend to affect, what it is they want done, and how they want to do it.

Those who set out to introduce a computer system should write out a detailed functional specification for that system. This step should be taken in conjunction with computing experts, perhaps employed as consultants. With the functional specification in hand, it will be possible to request tenders and/or to write more detailed hardware- and software-related specifications.

Before attacking the functional specification, we should fill in a gap we left earlier: the specification of system software. As with hardware, whatever is expected of or needed in terms of system software should also be laid out in a document.

THE SOFTWARE SPECIFICATION

It is not possible to fully detail a system software specification here. However, you should remember that before you choose a system, you must specify what kind of operating system is required (e.g., batch, time-shared, real-time); what the system should provide in terms of resources (e.g., input and output to terminals, access to secondary storage devices); what functions are needed (e.g., backup, security); and other considerations such as response time, method of use, etc.

Next, the required language(s) (e.g., FORTRAN, COBOL, BASIC) and the general speed and size characteristics of programs written in that language should be given. Whenever possible, specify a high-level language that will easily support future modifications to the program. The **documentation** expected should be stipulated. It should ideally include not only user manuals that show end-users how to employ the system software, but also a detailed description of its design and functions, together with listings of the source code. There should be no problem in demanding documentation if systems software is written by outside developers under contract specifically for a given use. However, when manufacturers or systems houses sell standard computer-system products to many users, they sometimes guard their investment in system software too jealously and refuse to supply detailed software documentation. In such circumstances there is little that a user can do for fear of violating the vendor's copyright, short of selecting another vendor who may possibly be more compliant.

Finally, the general kinds of application programs that the system will be required to support and as many specifics as possible about them should be detailed. If even partial examples exist, these should be made available so that the manufacturer or development company can see what is expected of their system in terms of the language and operating system capabilities required.

THE FUNCTIONAL SPECIFICATION

Now that we have looked at the hardware and software specifications for a system, we should note the following:

1. The hardware and software specifications can be put in their final form only by experts.
2. These specifications are completely dependent on what the system is to do — that is, what functions it is to perform.

What we need, then, is some clear, precise statement of what it is that the system is supposed to do for its users. This is the functional specification that must be developed with help from someone with previous experience by those who intend to employ the computer.

The functional-specification document should begin by describing the application area, the input that the users will bring to the system, and the output that is expected from the system. The maximum potential workload of the system and the maximum acceptable **turnaround time** (the time it takes between submitting input and obtaining relevant output) should be stated. Any **processing** (calculations, counts, etc.) of data should also be specified. In addition, details on what data is to be stored, how much is to be stored, how long it is to be stored, and how quickly it must be accessible should be stipulated. In other words, the functional specification for the whole computer system provides a detailed picture of the environment and of what the user wants the system to do. As such, it is a precise statement of what is expected of the system developer.

THE CONTRACT

Since the functional specification is the external description of the system, its terms should be written into a contract. If the system obtained is to be useful, it must be *at least* what the functional specification states. Therefore, if something does go wrong and you do not get what you wanted, you will have some recourse based on this specification. The precise way of writing such contracts cannot be covered here. However, you can find an understandable introduction to this field in a book by Brandon and Segelstein. [2] When the time comes to formalize the terms of a contract, legal counsel is obviously necessary. You would seek counsel if you were purchasing a house; you should do as much when buying a computer system.

Do not bank on the "goodwill" of the system vendor. *Never believe anything except what is written in a contract.* Persuasive advertising, verbal "guarantees," and unofficial correspondence mean absolutely nothing in the computer marketplace, as sad experience has revealed to many trusting neophytes. Be skeptical of vendors who try to sell you their computer solution even before they inquire about your specific problems.

When all decisions regarding the kind of system required for a particular application have been made, and when appropriate functional specifications have been laid down, it must then be determined how best to obtain the required system. At this point you can go to the marketplace with your functional specification to acquire a complete application system. Or with the help of experts you can develop hardware and system software specifications in order to buy a system on which development of your own applications package can be done. There are at least three alternatives in acquiring a system:

1. You can buy a prefabricated system and use it as is.
2. You can buy a prefabricated system and modify it.
3. You can assemble appropriate hardware and system software and write programs from scratch.

TURNKEY SYSTEMS

In some cases, there may be a turnkey system — a hardware and software package that some manufacturer has developed to serve precisely your kind of need. Turnkey systems can be the quickest way of getting a computer system into operation in a busy environment. When chosen carefully from a reputable supplier, such systems are — theoretically — greatly advantageous to the user.

Unfortunately, existing turnkey systems are seldom the working products that they are advertised to be. A review of even a few of the numerous examples of competing turnkey systems for the same applications will show that this is a tricky and potentially treacherous path to take.

In any applications area in which several vendors compete, a survey of existing turnkey systems will show which ones, if any, correspond to your functional specification. It is probable that no system will be precisely satisfactory, but a few might be close enough. Choosing the right one can be very difficult.

The probability that you will be able to obtain an "instant computer system" from a supplier is relatively small. At the very least, you will probably require some modification to an existing turnkey system before it will suit your individual needs. If you arrange for the original vendor to do this, the functional specification that has been written into a contract is all-important. If you decide to modify a turnkey system yourself, make sure that the original supplier (who owns the copyright on the software) will permit you to do so. When your own computer department starts modifying a vendor's product without written approval, the vendor may quite understandably void the product's warranties.

DO-IT-YOURSELF SYSTEMS

If you cannot buy a turnkey system to be used directly or modified, then it will be necessary for you to acquire the appropriate pieces of hardware and to get special software written for your particular application. You may arrange to have this done on a contract basis by an external developer, or you may have to use or establish your own in-house software-development group. If you do decide to go ahead on your own, then you must find the money and working space for the personnel you will need. You may have to be prepared to live with system-development personnel almost indefinitely, since the development process is sometimes lengthy. Frequently the requirements faced by a system may begin to change even before its first developement cycle is complete, "finished" may be a word seldom spoken.

SELECTING A SUPPLIER

The suppliers of computer systems (especially of the turnkey variety) work in several different ways. Some provide everything — hardware, systems software, and applications programs. More commonly, a **systems house** will buy hardware, an operating system, and languages from a computer manufacturer, and will supply only the applications programs as its own product. There are occasions, however, when systems houses even write their own versions of operating systems and languages.

What does the supplier's modus operandi imply for the user of the computer system? The overwhelming question you must answer before finally committing yourself to a particular supplier is this — can that supplier fully back up the system provided? The only way to answer this question is by doing your homework.

If the company supplying your system is also furnishing you with software, did its own staff write the software? If so, is the staff stationed at the local office? Nine times out of ten, the answer is no: The software was probably developed at a central office. You will often be surprised to learn (except with the larger companies) that there is no one capable of providing software maintenance located in your region, let alone in your city. If you deal with a local software house that writes its own programs, you will at least have someone accessible when you have complaints or modifications to propose.

Is the company offering to provide you with a system capable of hardware maintenance support? Do they have their own hardware-maintenance technicians, and do they keep spare parts on hand so that they can fix your system quickly when it breaks down? This is a critical consideration when the company is selling you a system composed of parts obtained from several different hardware suppliers.

If you are dealing with a company that has a local office assuming responsibility for all the hardware, software, and maintenance of the systems it provides, you are in much safer hands. If, on the other hand, a company with a small local bureau and a head office in Timbuktu hands you a "bargain" system born of a shotgun marriage of diverse hardware and software components, all provided by other companies that retain nominal responsibility for these parts — expect trouble! You may find yourself a wobbling domino that can be felled by the failure of any of several separate components in your "system." (See Fig. 11.1.)

COMPUTER PERSONNEL

Depending on the size and complexity of a computer application, the user will be exposed to a varying amount of contact with the people who develop computer systems. In the simplest case, he or she will consult appropriate experts who may find a company that already makes the needed computer product. Installation and user training for this new product may be a straightforward and brief matter. In the more complex case, there may be an in-house group dedicated to the development of new computer applications, or there may be a continuing relationship with a systems house. Either of these situations will involve new personnel and a longer time-base of interaction with the daily activities in the clinical environment. In the case of in-house development, computer personnel will be a new and expensive item in the budget.

Development Staff

Whether a computer application is developed in-house or by an outside agency, the skills of a number of people with distinct roles will have to be applied.

Fig. 11.1. The domino theory of computing
The more companies involved, the more likely a project is to fall on its face. Whenever possible, dealing with one company that assumes total system responsibility is preferred.

Before taking any definite steps in computing, a company or similar large institution may enlist the aid of **management consultants** and/or **data processing consultants** to help them discover the potential needs for data processing and its role in their environment. Once a real need and a definitive role for automation have been ascertained, any computer application will require a responsible, trained individual as a **project manager** during development. Often the "prime movers" who initiate computing projects seldom will have the time or expertise to properly manage even those projects that impact squarely in areas over which they maintain ultimate control. Therefore, an expert in computing may be called in to aid in the development of the system and to serve in the project management role.

The decision-making buck ultimately stops with the administrative staff who perceive problems and recognize that computers may help solve these problems. Their decisions, however, will be guided by those who have experience with the potential and limitations of computers. A large project may in itself justify the acquisition of such expertise.

In smaller applications, an external agency or group may be employed. If users whose individual projects are small can get together, they may be able to form a "critical mass" large enough to justify steps toward the establishment of a source of computer expertise and a shared computer system. Whatever the approach, seek help.

When software development actually begins, systems analysts will be working closely with the project manager or chief system developer. They will be responsible for the overall design strategy for attacking specific problem areas. In moderately large installations, "systems analyst" will usually be a job category in its own right. In smaller operations, the manager of the computing group may assume this role, or programmers (**programmer/analysts**) who are capable of doing systems analysis may be employed.

Those responsible for the actual **coding** (writing) of programs in a programming language and for the tactics involved in developing specific routines are computer programmers. There often is a senior or lead programmer who is responsible for immediate supervision and delegation of jobs among junior programmers. Programmers often assume responsibility for documenting software so that others can understand programs and change them later. Sometimes a developer will employ a professional documentation writer or a secretary for this purpose. Programming staff often do a poor job of documentation if left to their own resources. Since adequate documentation is vital to the survivability of any computer application, it is essential to make sure that this job is done properly.

Some or all of these people will be required for developing applications in-house. All of these roles will exist, but the number of people that fill them will vary with the size of the project, department, or organization. Departments or organizations may wish to retain outside systems-development groups with significant experience in the project(s) they are doing, especially if these projects are large and costly. However, organizations should never fail to have at least one person on their payroll who protects the organization's interests and who has appropriate responsibility.

Operational Staff

Even after a computer project leaves the development stage, your organization will need a creative expert to make system-related decisions. This person will be responsible for overseeing the system on a practical level and for assisting clinical personnel in formulating requests for changes to the system as necessary. The importance of the job of overseeing development and continuing growth of computers is reflected in a recent trend in the business world. It has become common for a business institution (where data processing is already an economically important area) to make a vice presidency of data processing a part of the administrative hierarchy. The message here is clear: Someone must be administratively responsible and the driver's seat must have one occupant.

Given a functioning computer system, somebody must turn it on, load tapes, and so on. These people are called **operators**. A big installation will have an operations supervisor who manages junior operators. In small installations — often the case in small businesses using minicomputers — programmers may absorb these roles, or there may be a part-time operator. Of course, when programmers are changing tapes, loading disks, and putting paper into the printer, they are not writing programs. The workload of the operator increases with the size and busyness of an installation.

Finally, **data-entry personnel** will be required to collect data and enter it into the computer. The importance of these people is often underrated. When you consider that the success of a computer application is totally dependent on these individuals for the quality of data input into the machine, your respect for them and their vital role in the system will be great. Sometimes it is possible to use a computer system to unburden existing secretarial or technical staff. These people can then be trained to become excellent data-entry personnel. If, however, no job role can be augmented by the computer, one must face up to the fact that a new job category has been created. Additional help will then be required if data is ever to get into the computer.

When a computer installation assumes responsibility for continuing program modification and development of new programs, the development personnel mentioned above (analysts and programmers) will have permanent roles in that organization. Despite the continuing role of these individuals in applications programming, a software maintenance contract must always be arranged with the original developer. This contract will ensure that the developer continues to provide corrections for errors and the latest versions of system software (the operating system and the programming language updates). Software-maintenance contracts are expensive, but they cannot be ignored simply because in-house applications programmers are employed. In general, for maintenance you must depend on the company that supplied the system software.

GETTING GOING

It is not easy to implement any worthwhile computer system. A rapid and painless transition may mean only that the computer system being introduced is so unimportant that it has no discernible effect on its environment.

The best break-in procedure is to run manual and automated systems in parallel until the automated system is running smoothly enough that manual procedures can be stopped. It is difficult to be sure that a program is performing exactly as designed and that it is free of bugs. Manual procedures, therefore, should never be totally abandoned. Some alternative way of performing your task will be necessary when the computer system fails because of some obscure software error previously undetected, or because of mechanical or electrical breakdown (a frequent occurrence). It is surprising how many turnkey systems are sold without formal backup procedures ever being specified. When disaster eventually strikes, the need is acutely perceived but little can be done. If only the School of Hard Knocks had an extension program so that everyone could appreciate the problem without having to go through a disaster!

Put simply, backup procedures fall into two categories:

1. Manual procedures that permit an operation to continue while the computer is unavailable.
2. Computer procedures that will enable the computer system to "recover" from any disruption that its failure might have caused.

Automatic procedures for backup include periodic printing of cumulative paper documents (permitting support of manual procedures and the collection of data transacted during the period the system is down); the regular copying of all data onto spare disk packs or tapes (preventing the complete loss of data stored on secondary-storage devices if they fail); and the redundant recording of all data transactions on another magnetic medium (often tape) — a process called transaction logging or journaling. If a system fails, data can be collected on manual forms and reports can be produced manually. When the computer is again operational, the last copy of the data kept on secondary storage can be loaded onto the system (if the original was destroyed) and the transaction log can be used to "play-back" to the system everything that happened up to the point of destruction of the data. Then, the only data that must be entered by hand will be the data collected during down time. These **fail-soft** procedures will eventually pay off in every installation and will enable a failed computer system to be brought back "**up**" with a minimum of work.

However, when a system must be available all the time, the only way to approach 100-percent availability is to acquire redundant hardware. Any given piece of computer hardware will fail sooner or later, so even the CPU itself may have to be duplicated and even a tandem system may have to be considered in some critical applications. Even a one-percent down-time per year means that 20 hours might be lost per year during the day shift alone. One should also realize that beyond such unscheduled down-time, there are also normal computer "housekeeping" activities (such as doing backup) that will usually remove the computer from user service at least a few hours per week.

MONITORING PROGRESS

Once installed, a computer system will go through phases in its life cycle. From time to time, parts of it, such as specific items of hardware or particular programs, may need replacement or expansion in order to cope with increasing workloads or changing applications. Such replacement or expansion of programs has been called software maintenance, and it often represents *50–80 percent of the ultimate investment* in any program package.

Certain landmarks in the life course of a system should be envisioned during the planning stages, if possible, and defined courses of action should be followed when each landmark is passed. Included in these checkpoints should be the signs and symptoms indicating when a computer application is no longer meeting needs and should be improved, or when it is obsolete and should be dismantled or replaced. The failure to consider growth and change will eventually result in a computer system that is only an end in itself — costing everyone and serving no one.

CONCLUSIONS

For good or ill, a computer system will substantially alter your way of "doing business." Often a whole department or institution will change in the process of accommodating a computer. This is not necessarily bad if a rational approach is taken and you foresee and plan for the effects.

But you should be an agent of change *before* a system is installed. It is ridiculous and sometimes impossible to automate a mess, so a serious effort needs to be made to clean up procedures before introducing automation. Automation involves more than merely "computerizing" (a hateful word!) the status quo. Before committing any operation to a computer and facing the concomitant cost, one should take the opportunity afforded by the advent of automation to improve, adjust, and reorganize existing procedures in order to eliminate waste and redundancy.

Consider also the people who will make the system work, use it, and maintain it. Every person who works with a computer system, however indirectly, is part of that system and will therefore be affected by it. Each person should be aware that he or she will also, conversely, affect the system. You should take care to ensure that staff do not feel alienated or threatened by the new computer in their midst. Listen to people's fears: Take time to show them how they fit into the new computer-based system as surely as they fit into the old manual one. Often, in fact, their roles will be enhanced in a properly implemented system.

Obviously, then, one should study the impact of a computer system on an environment and be fully aware of its effects before proceeding. It is unrealistic and self-deceptive to pretend that the introduction of a computer system will be painless, cheap, or totally satisfactory. No system is ever fully satisfactory to all its users. Inevitably there will be unrealistic or conflicting demands that have been or will be made on it.

One of the most frequently made and least frequently kept demands made on computer systems is that they should save money. Many systems acclaimed as economically "in the black" are made to appear that way by people who conveniently ignore some of the costs associated with them. It is very difficult, especially in a nonprofit-oriented organization, to use computers to save money, especially if they are not incorporated "whole hog" into an operation and are instead just "add-ons." A more realistic hope for most computer systems is that they earn their keep in situations where the work load is expanding and where the projected increase in staff can be eliminated or reduced. The computer can absorb additional work, thereby containing costs at a certain level. These financial facts often come as both a surprise and a disappointment to users who approach the use of computer systems full of blind faith created by sales pitches.

After the early blush of enthusiasm, the naive user will often find a computer system to be significantly less than originally anticipated. An inevitable let-down ensues. It is a dreadful blow for the average user to realize that this marvelous new computer equipment will not fulfill every fantasy. Seasoned systems developers tend to ignore complaining clients until the clients become acquainted with the things that the system *can* do. There is a real danger, though, that the prevailing gloom of the unprepared users may deepen into permanent disgust. At this point they may throw out the baby with the bath water and radically change automation priorities for no particularly good reason. The user frustrated by a new computer system might do well to ponder the example of the credulous child enraged at the family dog because it refuses to talk. Serious developers will prepare users early for this problem, and make sure that they understand and appreciate both immediate and long-term constraints. The mature user will be able to weather the initial phase and will be able to face the facts of what the computer can and cannot do.

Those unfamiliar with the potential and the limitations of systems in relation to their particular problems can seek the opinion and assistance of experts.

The system chosen by amateurs frequently serves not their needs, but those of the computer supplier. Ill-considered acquisitions are often abandoned once they are perceived as useless. Alternatively and much worse, it is not unknown for a computer system's sponsor to throw lots of good money after bad in order to keep his or her reputation in shape. Some sound initial vectoring and a few mid-course maneuvers from an expert may save you from such a fate.

Stripped of their mystery, aura, and the erroneous notion that they can solve every problem, computer systems emerge as basically a mixture of hardware, software, and people — a combination that acts as just another useful tool in your armamentarium.

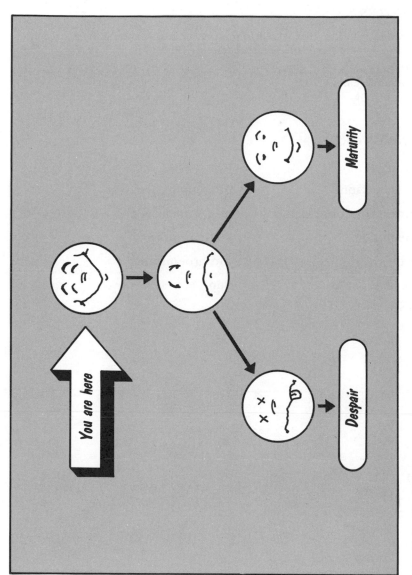

Fig. 11.2. Pilgrim's progress
The brand-new computer user, enthusiastic at first, is quickly disillusioned. This disappointment can proceed either to hopeless despair or to mature appreciation of the limitations and potentials of computer systems.

NOTES

1. F. Lustman, P. Lanthier, D. Charbonneau, et. al., A systematic approach to choosing a computer. *Canadian Datasystems* 10:4:24 (April) 1978.

2. D. H. Brandon, and S. Segelstein, *Data Processing Contracts*. New York: Van Nostrand-Reinhold, 1976.

NEW WORDS

coding

data-entry person

data processing consultant

documentation

fail-soft

management consultant

operator

processing

programmer/analyst

project manager

systems house

turnaround time

"up"

12

Through the Computer, Darkly

Straining on the Tether of Technology

In preceding chapters we have seen that each component in a computer system has its own set of limitations. In the case of hardware, these limits are usually technological in nature — sometimes the devices we would like to have do not yet exist. The limits of software engineering are manifested in the difficulties encountered in programming computers and in implementing systems capable of dealing with humans on human terms. Workers in computer system development are constantly straining on the tether of existing computer technology. It often happens that the human mind can imagine a perfect, completed computer system that is ideally suited to cope with some problem. But in reality, the severe constraints imposed by the facts of current technology usually stop us short of our goals. When the ideal system that we want does not exist, we are then forced to accept real substitutes that are usually disappointing in comparison to our "dream systems."

When the uninitiated think of computers, they frequently imagine a magical machine that refines murky, raw data into crystal-clear information. In fact, the converse is often true. Use of a computer system to process information can distort, coarsen, and veil that information. The output that we obtain from computers is but a dark and shadowy image of the reality we attempt to represent to them, and this is an important (though hidden) problem affecting the application of computers.

In attempts to apply computers to specific problems, the sheer limitations of systems technology can frustrate even the most optimistic of developers and users. Since computers cannot communicate the same way people do, people must transform information to suit the computer. Humans must adopt strange procedures, languages, and formats to input data. Similarly, when seeking information from a computer, people must accept it in the format and on the media that the machine offers.

People who approach computing with unrealistically high

expectations and little appreciation of the boundaries of the state of the art are certain to be disillusioned. In an effort to prevent such disappointments, let us therefore consider the problems posed by a computer reality that usually lags far behind our fondest dreams.

THE UNREALITY OF COMPUTER "MEMORY"

Consider the page you are reading. You can see and touch it. If the ink is new, perhaps you can even smell it. This page is part of our world. We are used to encountering information with our entire sensorium. The more senses employed, the more complete the contact is and the better we learn.

Suppose you just scan this chapter now but want to read it in detail later. There will be a number of methods for locating it. You can be compulsive and keep a card index. It is probably more likely, however, that you will remember it as being in the book with such-and-such a cover; or you may recall having put it in a particular place or having borrowed it from a certain person. Your idiosyncratic scheme of sensory cues would help you find the chapter with a minimum of rummaging.

Information in tangible, physical form is easy to handle. But let us now consider the case of information going directly into a computer. In this process, the physical context of the data is stripped off. When you want to review the data (i.e., get output on a CRT terminal), no physical cues will be associated with it. Later, when you try to retrieve the data, you will not be much helped by your first encounter with it, since the data never was in any context which would serve as an *aide-mémoire*.

Unfortunately for us, there is no computer memory device that possesses the associative power of the human brain. A computer's secondary storage can perhaps hold more precise numeric detail than the human brain usually can. However, contrary to popular belief, we often have a great deal of difficulty in retrieving the items that the machine has "remembered." Computers are incapable of providing data on the basis of imprecise requests. They cannot find the information stored away in their memory banks unless some human has told them exactly how to find it.

Thus, to use computers effectively, we are forced to index information thoroughly — random rummaging, cue association, and approximate locating are in general not possible. Although putting data on the computer system should be done to achieve a definitive benefit, the price that one pays can be high: Direct contact with the information can be lost.

After all, where does the data go? Not into the red binder. Not into the old filing cabinet, or onto the shelf. For all practical human purposes, the data leaves our sensory world. We have thrown our data across a chasm between our world and the world of the computer where information is represented as electronic signals and magnetic fields. We cannot see it, touch it, or hope to find it again if it is misfiled.

It is therefore not surprising that nomcomputer scientists might feel insecure about casting their lot with computers. Important financial data dare not be lost. Research data may have taken months to gather, and one is justifiably possessive of it. Paper records are physically reassuring. On the other hand, the assurance by a priest of the computer cult that your data is alive and well on a spinning disk is intellectually acceptable, but requires considerable faith. It is possible to see your data, providing that the system is available when you want it. Even then, however, insecurity can persist. The light patterns on a cathode-ray tube are transient representations of your hard-earned data. To be truly assured, one is inclined to seek printed output. Again we turn to our paper security-blanket.

"Computerization" of data, then, is by no means a panacea for the ills besetting information availability. Actually, the very fact that data does reside in a computer implies a certain level of added expense, artificial formalization, and insecurity that cannot be ignored.

LIMITATIONS OF THE INPUT PROCESS
Information retrieval, however, is only one area in which our use of computers is constrained by the current state of the art. The very process of inputting data into that memory imposes even more stringent limitations.

We might understand this more by asking a pointed question: Why don't all computer scientists automate their literature files? Why do some of them use cards and a recipe box for a literature index, while others have no organized system at all? An automated-literature index could provide definite benefits such as a list of key words and quick access to abstracts and subjective notes. There are a number of reasons why this is not often done.

1. It is often expensive to interact with computers since a terminal usually costs $1000 or more.
2. A terminal is usually too heavy to carry about.
3. Portable terminals require access to a telephone wherever they are used, and hand-held terminals are extremely rare and limited. So far, a wireless hand-held terminal is scarcely more than a novelty. Until sufficient technological evolution occurs, Mohammed must continue to go to the mountain (or at least to the terminal room) to get his computing done.
4. Almost all terminals are based on typing input, and none understand speech or handwriting.
5. Since computers cannot read books, getting data into a computer system is a lot of work. Ultimately, the effort of organizing and preparing the material would probably not be perceived as worthwhile.

In light of the fact that "insiders" don't automate their literature files, it is small wonder that automation of other kinds of information has found limited acceptance — especially since even larger amounts of information are usually involved.

Another aspect should be considered. To human beings, reality is a continuum. Although we want to input to a computer information that represents reality, the computer requires that we classify, categorize, and quantize the data (break it into a finite number of categories) before it can be processed in any way. Computers cannot cope with human reality. Instead, categories must be imposed on the information.

There are two ways of getting information into computer-processable form. One way is to input everything as it is into the computer, and then to write programs that carry out the quantization process. This approach has worked only in very limited areas — such as the processing of pathology reports — because it is extremely difficult for computers to dissect the structure and meaning of human-readable text and because the input of large quantities of undigested information requires much effort. So until computers learn to read books and journals as people can, inputting everything will often be too expensive, even in those rare cases in which it is technically possible.

The more common approach is to quantize data before putting it into a computer. This process of encoding data into categories based on explicit criteria has been called "taxonorics." [1, 2] Taxonorics represents an attempt to define a precise way of stuffing continuous reality into computer-compatible pigeon-holes, while distorting reality as little as possible. (See Fig. 12.1.)

Collecting and condensing information before input usually forces the interposition of a coding clerk between the information source and the computer. This often leads to delays and to transcription errors. Frequently special forms must be provided for gathering data. Even when properly designed, these forms themselves can be a source of errors. [3] Obviously errors can occur even if the individual at the source personally encodes the information, since different people may have different interpretations of supposedly standard terms. When the data is finally ready to be entered into a computer system, errors may occur during the input device's reading of computer-compatible media (such as OMR or OCR forms), and in further typing steps if they are needed. Many errors can occur in a data collection and input process. (See Fig. 12.2.) The propensity for errors has resulted in extensive research on their prevention, detection, and correction. [4]

Clearly, there is no point in putting data into a computer unless it is to be used to generate output. The cost of input virtually demands that computer-based records become a vital and active part of any enterprise. This high cost prevents the computer from simply replacing a record that has become a useless pro forma repository of observations — often the fate of paper documents. If you are not

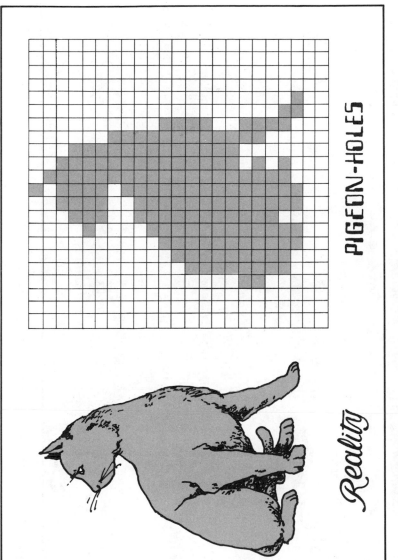

Fig. 12.1. Stuffing reality into computer-compatible pigeon-holes

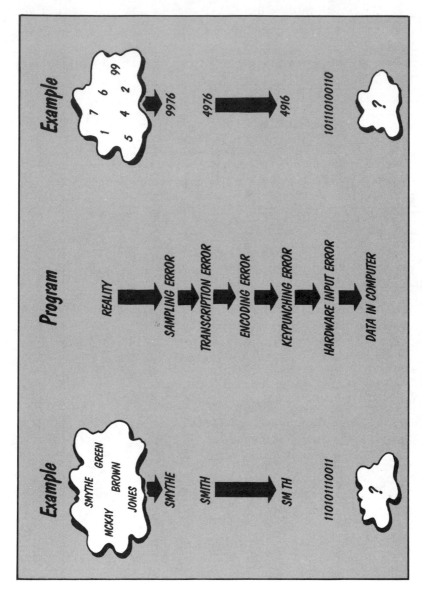

Fig. 12.2.   How data collection becomes garbage collection

really using a computer to its fullest, then it is using you and you should trade it in on a filing cabinet and a few clerks.

HOW OUTPUT CRAMPS OUR STYLE

We have considered the input process as a limiting feature in computer applications, but input is only half of the two-way channel between users and the computer. In what ways do hardware and software inhibit the full realization of the potential of computer systems in the output process?

Output technology is not always available when and where we want it. Terminals are often inaccessible, or at least not easily available to the business person who is constantly on the move. Even when terminals are available, standing in line to use them is unacceptable; yet the more terminals, the greater the cost.

Furthermore, the format of computer output often leaves a great deal to be desired. It can be cramped, styleless, voluminous, and inscrutable. It may be difficult to extract important items since most printers print only in one color and since often it is difficult to underline or otherwise highlight parts of the output.

Another problem is determined by the limitations of the programs we know how to write: Our systems lack the ability to select only data of interest or significance for output. We have not yet found ways to turn computer systems into information integrators. They are not currently capable of reliably extracting salient features of data, although advanced research is beginning to probe this area.

Even if these obstacles are overcome, we may not get the output we want — only the output someone else wanted us to have.

Budget, expediency, or ignorance of available alternatives may also create constraints, especially regarding the speed and the availability of graphic output. Long waits for slowly typed output, or the hard-to-read, poorly aligned, capitals-only character set of some line printers, undermine user acceptance of any system. Providing columns of numbers instead of graphics fails to use the computer's ability to manipulate and represent information in more digestible and condensed form. The superiority of pictures over words and numerals has long been appreciated. In reviewing some computer implementations, one is left with the conviction that developers were unaware of present-day output technology.

A further and critical problem associated with computer output is that people accept it on blind faith. They won't believe newspapers, they doubt what's said on TV, but they do trust computers for some unknown reason. They assume that something produced by a computer must be correct. Nonsense! This is about as valid as believing everything in a book because it was produced on a printing press. People generate and enter data, and write programs to process that data. People make mistakes. Computer programs can be based on human misconceptions, or programs can be affected by human problems in mapping our conceptions into the simple steps of which computers are capable. People who are uncritical of computer output are guilty of the ultimate buck-passing. It is the human's responsibility to question computer output, because the computer isn't programmed to "question" itself. Errors often may live forever undetected; whereas a human may at least harbor a spark of doubt about human output, the computer will never question its own errors.

Perhaps the greatest of all problems mentioned above is one not determined by input and output devices, but rather by the inability of current systems (especially their programs) to distill the essence out of masses of data. To take a case in point, if we walk into a board room and ask, "How is the company doing?" the comptroller may reply, "Fine." This person may have formulated a judgment based on masses of data, but with all irrelevant particulars excluded. Computers cannot in general make such qualitative evaluations because they seldom contain models for economic processes. A person seeking information from most computer systems could get lots of data but no succinct response. On the other hand, the reassuring impression we got about the company may not have been based on all available data, and in this respect decisions based on the output of a computer system that collected exhaustive data might be more sound.

The inability of computers to comprehend relationships among multiple pieces of data is evident in medical monitoring systems in which alarms are often based on single parameters deviating from a specified range. Bells, buzzers, or beepers can sound constantly instead of only at those points where there is truly a clinical turn for the worse. Unless a program has been developed that meaningfully integrates multiple parameters and makes a judgment, an alarm is really nothing more than a befuddled request by the equipment for a human to evaluate the situation. Too many false alarms will ultimately lead to ignoring or disabling the alarm system. A failure to recognize a deteriorating trend among several parameters, any one of which may still be within the arbitrary "normal" range, is even more sinister since staff can be lulled into a false sense of security.

Another thought experiment relating to this area is to consider the sense of vision. Seeing involves two levels of acuity. Centrally we see sharply and in high detail. Peripheral vision has lower resolution. We can concentrate on an object, yet be aware of its context. This ability to keep detail and context together is still a matter for research as far as computers are concerned.

COMMUNICATIONS — GRAND DESIGNS, PALE REALITY

It is sometimes said that the future of computer technology lies in great networks of interconnected computers that could share data in a vast, distributed "data bank." On a smaller scale, networks of computers encompassing several company branch offices could be useful for a variety of services and collaborative endeavors.

However, the "ease" with which we can communicate with remote computers and they with each other cannot be taken for granted. In the simplest case — connecting a remote, portable terminal to a central computer — even the use of an ordinary acoustic coupler is not perfectly convenient. A telephone is required, and noise on the line can and does sometimes interfere with data transmission. The modest data-transmission speed achievable with these devices also leaves something to be desired. This speed cannot be much improved unless one is willing to sacrifice portability to install another more permanent communications device.

Because they are much grander communications schemes, networks have correspondingly greater limitations associated with them. Hardware cost, speed restrictions, and incompatible communications protocols may all severely limit the benefits we can extract from communications technology in our computer system.

THE HUMAN FACTOR

Just as hardware and software technologies impose limits on computer systems, so also those who develop and use these systems impose their own human limitations. The finite nature of the human factor is reflected in the computing projects of these individuals — specifically in the large number of failures.

Most people are surely optimists by nature. Characteristically we believe that diligent effort must ultimately be rewarded by discovery and progress. If we did not believe this, most of us would draw the logical inference from the observation that our work seldom produces dramatic results, and take up permanent residence under a coconut tree!

Therefore, we tend to welcome hopefully any tool that promises to help us in our various pursuits. Those who earn their living by selling computers have been quick to exploit our optimism, and the resulting ballyhoo about "the computer solution" leads many people to believe that proved and reliable computer products exist for many problematic areas. In reality, few such products are available. Many computer systems are often "one-off" prototypes — not reliable, tested products. Fact seldom measures up to fancy.

The failure of people to appreciate the true limitations of technological advances has been demonstrated time and time again. For example, we are presently living with the sober reality that has displaced the initial enthusiasm of the scientific community for atomic energy. Remember the days when we were told that there would be enough nuclear fuel to serve the world's energy needs cheaply, safely, and forever? Those were optimistic times. Nobody thought that we would ever be running low on nuclear fuel. Few envisioned that nuclear-power plants might contaminate our environment. Nor did anyone consider the horrifying prospect that any banana republic with a nuclear reactor might be able to manufacture atomic weapons.

In the heady days just after World War II, popular-science magazines assured us that by 1980 we would all be flying our own airplanes to work. Our communities, they prophesied, would consist of long rows of houses with roads at the front door and airstrips at the back door. So much for our ability to map scientific theory into the real world!

In an analogous manner, people who imagine that computer systems will soon solve all their problems are usually victims of false optimism. In system development the tendency of the human mind to leap in a single bound from lowly reality to an idealized concept without considering the boundary between them is a reef on which many a computing project has foundered.

Most informed people these days are aware that computers are obstinate machines that require explicit programs in order to function. We draw from this knowledge the obvious conclusion that unless we thoroughly understand a process, nobody can program a computer to imitate that process. Most areas in which we might wish to use computers are not nearly the "hard" or purely scientific disciplines that computer professionals might wish them to be. In many cases we cannot express what we are doing in logical sequence — because we truly do not know how we work. We draw on a variable store of information, past experience, educated guesses, and intuition to make judgments and formulate plans. (Some of us are better than others in this respect.) We recognize that often other people may make different choices based on the same information. No one could begin to state in detail how a "universal" person assesses data, so naturally no computer programmer can do this either. The limits of our understanding of the human processes at work in thinking strictly circumscribe the ways in which we can use computers to support it!

On Creativity

Just as an overactive imagination can be the user's biggest limitation, so an underactive imagination can cause system developers to impose their own artificial limits on the potential of existing technology.

The single biggest problem in this respect is caused by the uncreative developer who is content to "computerize" an existing process. Sometimes, considerable modification of a process is needed in order to "tune" it properly before automation should even be contemplated. Even more significantly, if computers are to be used to advance our social systems, then surely we ought to employ them to do things that we are presently not able to do without their help. The developer who stumbles about seeking existing projects to automate may be missing the most important potential benefits of automation.

A truly creative person with an adequate background in both computer science, and with the ability to see things that never were but that might be achieved in an application, is still a rare find. A computer programmer can code a program, but it takes a skilled analyst to know what program to write. The limited availability of high-level, innovative personnel imposes yet another restriction on our use of computers.

A SERIES OF HURDLES

Although it may at first appear necessary and possible to automate a given application, the sheer cost of technology may be a first impenetrable barrier to actual implementation. If this is not the case, then the success and utility of an implementation may trip over any of several more hurdles. We must include here the constraints caused by the rather simple ways in which those devices we know as computers can process information. We find it extremely difficult to program them to do some of the things that people find easy: using associative reasoning; retrieving relevant past experience; distilling intelligence from masses of data; and leaping intuitively to or guessing intelligently at solutions to complex problems. Part of the reason for this is that the programming tools available to us are still fairly difficult to use and restricted in scope. A more fundamental limitation, however, is that we don't really understand what is involved in many of our activities well enough to write programs to imitate them.

If we come to grips with this reality, we must finally cope with the somewhat "primitive" technology available to input and store information in a computer, and to obtain output from it as well. The possibility of employing automation in situations where potential benefits would seem to accrue is often blocked by the devices that must be used. Until we have input devices that can read books, accept scribbled notes, and listen to speech, we will have difficulties in getting much of day-to-day reality into a system. Until we have reasonably inexpensive output devices that can produce highlighted, graphical, and even verbal output, we will be constrained in using them.

Computer memory with the versatility and associative power of human memory is not available in any form. Devices and software that permit computers to be interconnected in networks are still expensive and restricted in capability.

All of these factors limit the use of computers in the service of humankind, at least for the present. For now, only partial solutions exist. Therefore we must settle for second best and cunningly design systems that help as much as possible in spite of these substantial limitations.

NOTES

1. A. R. Feinstein, Taxonorics I: formulation of criteria. *Arch. Intern. Med.* 126:679, 1970.

2. A. R. Feinstein, Taxonorics II: formats and coding systems for data processing. *Arch. Intern. Med.* 126:1053, 1970.

3. D. E. Seager, The ten commandments of forms design. *Canadian Datasystems* 9:9:40 (October) 1977.

4. I. K. Crain, Entry and validation of scientific data — how to prevent "garbage in." *Infor.* 15:160, 1977.

Glossary

Words in the explanations that are themselves defined in this glossary are printed in **boldface**.

For other, more complete sources of definitions of data processing terms, see the following:

1. A. Chandor; J. Graham; and R. Williamson, *A Dictionary of Computers.* London: Penguin, 1970.
2. A. Ralston and C. L. Meek, *Encyclopedia of Computer Science.* New York: Petrocelli/Charter, 1976.

Access To retrieve information from some **storage device** such as **internal memory**, disk, or tape. The *access time* is the time it takes to locate data, retrieve it, and place it in a **register** where it can be operated on. The access time for data in **internal memory** is usually 1 μsec or less, whereas for disk it is typically greater than 10–15 msec. See also **Random Access Memory**.

Acoustic Coupler A device for changing a sequential train of pulses, corresponding to a **binary** number, into sounds of a given frequency, which are piped into the mouthpiece of a standard telephone set for transmission to a remote telephone receiver. The reverse process is achieved by changing the received sounds back into a train of pulses.

Address The numerical designation given to a memory **location**.

Algorithm Sequences of logical steps that carry out specific **tasks**, operations, and transformations of data. An exact description of the solution to a problem.

Analog Computers Computers that perform operations on continuous signals. Their output is in the form of continuous signals such as voltage fluctuations, waveforms, etc.

Analog-to-Digital Converter An **input device** for changing continuous physical (analog) signals into digital form, i.e., discrete numbers. A *digital-to-analog converter* does the opposite and has application in electronic and electromechanical **output devices**.

Applications Package A self-contained collection of **programs** designed to serve some specific set of requirements (an application). A good commercial example would be the SPSS statistics package that is sold as a unit.

Applications Program A **program**, written by users or supplied by a company, that serves a particular need or set of needs. Examples of an applications program would be a program to generate a specific report, a program to perform a particular set of calculations, etc. Most of the time, a high-level **programming language** is used.

Arithmetic Unit That part of the **central processing unit** that carries out arithmetic operations such as add, subtract, increment, decrement, etc.

Assembler A **programming language** that allows the use of mnemonic codes for machine instructions and symbols for variables, which are then processed and turned into **machine language**.

Asynchronous In *asynchronous transmission,* data is sent one **character** at a time, and the time of arrival of characters at the receiver is arbitrary. See Fig. 6.2.

Backup The process of creating a computer-compatible duplicate of information stored on a **computer system**. Also the procedure for redundant recording of information. *Backup hardware* usually refers to a duplicate or equivalent of any **peripheral device** or of the computer itself. *Backup procedure* usually refers to a procedure, ordinarily paper-based, for manually recording and managing information during a system failure.

Bar Code One of a variety of schemes for representing numerical or alphanumerical (letters and number digits) sequences, typically as black strips of varied width and spacing. One variation of these appears on many consumer packages.

Batch Operating System   For an adequately detailed explanation of this topic, see the section entitled "A Means of Sharing" in Chapter 9.

Binary   Refers to numbers of the base 2. Such numbers can be composed of only the digits 0 and 1: numbers are thus strings of 0s and 1s, in which each digit position toward the left represents an increasing power of 2. The number "101" (101_2) is read from the right to left as $(1 \times 2^0) + (0 \times 2^1) + (1 \times 2^2) = (1 + 0 + 4) = 5_{10}$. Computers use binary numbers because such numbers are easy to represent as on and off states in simple circuits and because they are easy to process, since rules for logical and arithmetic operations in the base 2 can be implemented in simple circuits.

Bit   Constructed from the words **BI**nary digi**T**, the term refers to a single digit of a **binary** number. For example, the binary number 101 is composed of three bits.

Bug   An unintentional error in a **program**. See also **debugging**.

Bundled   Refers to the fact that the cost of the **software** is included in the overall price of a **computer system**. This often means that the software cannot be obtained separately. (Cf. **unbundled**.)

Byte   The number of **bits** required to encode one **character** of information in any given **computer system**. In most **minicomputers**, two bytes of eight bits each form one **word**.

Cathode Ray Tube (CRT)   An electronic tube (of which the familiar television picture tube is an example), in which an electron beam is deflected in patterns and hits a phosphor, which makes its output visible to a human. Sometimes called a *VDU,* for *visual display unit.*

Central Processing Unit (CPU)   The part or parts of computer **hardware** that carry out data manipulation (**processing** or moving data) and control the sequence of operations performed by the computer. One important part of the CPU is the arithmetic unit, which performs arithmetic. Another part is the control unit that supervises the sequencing of operations. The **internal memory** contains the **instructions (programs)** that determine what is to be done and in what sequence.

Channel   A pathway for data into or out of a **computer system**. Usually it is made up of multiple parallel wires, each of which transfers one **bit** of a **byte** or **word** simultaneously.

Character Any letter, digit, or punctuation mark. Characters are usually represented by a **binary** code composed of eight or nine **bits**. Such a code,and any piece of information eight or nine bits in length, is usually referred to as a **byte**.

Coding The process of representing information in some other form. To encode data involves changing it from one form such as decimal to another form such as **binary**. To "decode" data means to change it back from encoded to original form. When referring to a **program**, "coding" refers to the action of writing the programs in a given **programming language**.

Compiler A **program** that translates human-readable **source code** into more machine-like **object code**. The object code may be an intermediate code to be further translated into **machine language**, or it may actually be machine language.

Computer Usually refers to an entire **computer system** (the **processor** plus all **peripheral devices**). Actually it should refer only to the **central processing unit**, although it may also include **internal memory**.

Computer-Aided Instruction (CAI) The use of a **computer system** in education. In medical training, computers have been used to provide multiple-choice quizzes or even to simulate patients or physiological systems.

Computer Output Microfilm (COM) A device for producing photographic film output directly from a computer. Such devices are very high-speed, often using an electron beam on a **cathode ray tube** to produce light patterns that can be recorded on film.

Computer System This always refers to the entire **hardware** package and would most properly include all **software** as well. The emphasis here is on a working whole.

Control Unit That part of the **central processing unit** that directs the sequence of operations, such as which **instruction** is to be **executed** next.

Cylinder On a disk pack, a cylinder is a stack of **tracks**, all of which are equidistant from the central axle. In a disk pack, the nth cylinder consists of the nth track on each surface of every platter. Since the **read/write** heads of a disk pack are ganged, it increases efficiency to store related data on cylinders so that all data can be read without having to reposition the heads.

Data Access Arrangement (DAA) A mechanism sometimes required by the telephone company that goes between a device and the telephone line on which the device will transmit or receive. Its claimed purpose is to prevent electrical damage to the telephone system.

Data Definition Language (DDL) A special group of commands used in database management systems that allows the definition of the structure and contents of the database.

Data Entry Clerk A staff person whose role is to transcribe or to input data directly into a computer via some **input device.**

Data Management Language (DML) A group of commands that give a **programmer** a standard method of storing and retrieving data when using a database system.

Data Processing Consultant An expert in the use of computers in specific applications environments, e.g., business data processing consultant, medical data processing consultant.

Dataset See **modem.**

Debugging The process of discovering and correcting errors in **programs.**

Digital Computer A device that performs calculations and manipulates data composed of discrete elements such as numbers. Most modern digital computers work in the **binary** number system.

Diskette Sometimes called *floppy disks* or *flexible disks.* A diskette is an oxide-coated, flexible-plastic, magnetic recording **medium. Access** time is slow — often exceeding 100 msec, and capacity is small — usually less than one **Mb.** However, diskettes are relatively inexpensive.

Distributed Processing Refers to the utilization of a mix of local and remote computer power, available for the solution of a user's problem.

Documentation *User documentation:* an instruction manual or its equivalent that provides users with sufficient information to use a system. *System documentation:* description of **hardware** and **software,** contained in a variety of manuals. *Program documentation:* a concise, complete exposé of what a **program** does and how it does it, on both an overall basis and a detailed basis. Documentation is most important when someone other than the original **programmer** must correct or extend a program.

Dot Matrix A method of producing **characters** for viewing by either brightening or darkening an appropriate combination of dots in a two-dimensional array. Most dot matrix representations are 5 horizontal points X 7 vertical points, or 7 horizontal X 9 vertical.

Down; Down-Time Period of time during which a **computer system** is not functioning. *Scheduled down time* is the time during which the system is not available, not because it has failed but because it is performing functions such as **backup,** or because preventive **hardware** maintenance is being done. *Unscheduled down time:* unexpected system failure.

Drive A mechanical mechanism on which a magnetic secondary-storage **medium** is mounted to make its data accessible to the computer, e.g., disk drive or tape drive. A drive contains all electrical and mechanical components necessary to **read** or **write** data on its medium but it often excludes its controller, which controls the flow of data between the computer and the drive.

Dumb Terminal A **terminal** that does not possess any intrinsic data processing capability and that acts as a pure **input** and/or **output device.**

Execute To perform the operation indicated by an **instruction.** If the instruction is "add," to execute "add" is to carry out the addition. To execute a **program,** a computer does what is specified by the instructions that make up the program.

Fail-Soft Describes a mechanism that permits a **computer system** to continue in operation, although at a reduced capacity and/or with reduced **resources,** after a failure of part of the system.

Firmware **Instructions, routines,** and **programs** that today are typically implemented in **read only memory (ROM)** and are available for **execution** but not for alteration.

Floppy Disk See **diskette.**

Flow Charting A graphical representation (by using blocks and arrows) of the logical sequence of **execution** of a **program.**

Full Duplex Refers to the ability of a communications linkage to send and to receive simultaneously on the same line.

Gb (Gigabyte) One billion **bytes.** 1000 **Mb.**

Half Duplex A communications linkage that can send and receive — but not simultaneously. Sometimes the term *simplex* is used for a linkage that can only send *or* receive.

Hard Copy Any human-readable output from a computer that is produced on paper or other permanent media.

Hardware The physical devices included in a **computer system**.

Hard-Wired Physically (and usually permanently) connected to a computer, usually by an electronic conductor. *Hard-wired programs:* on old computers, **programs** actualized in the form of interconnections of wires on **patchboards**. A method still used on **analog computers** to process continuous signals instead of digital (numerical) information.

Input Device A machine capable of accepting data and making it available for **processing** in a form acceptable to a computer.

Instruction One of the fundamental operations that can be performed by a computer, e.g., "add."

Intelligent Terminal A computer peripheral that, in addition to providing input/output facilities, also allows some processing and often storage of data. Intelligent terminals can sometimes operate in a stand-alone mode (not connected to any other computer) for the purpose of data collection. When a data collection session is complete, the terminal can then be connected to the main computer and the data can be transferred from the intelligent terminal to the main computer.

Internal Memory The storage facilities in a **computer system** where **programs** and data are placed immediately before **execution**. It is usually the highest-speed memory on a computer system, although sometimes small higher-speed *cache memories* are made part of the internal memory.

Interpreter A **program** that translates the statements written in some **programming language** and **executes** them one statement or group of statements at a time. No **object code** is produced.

Interpreting Using a special version of a **keypunch** machine to print in human-readable form across the top of **punched cards** the information that is represented by their punched holes.

Joystick A device for inputting X-Y coordinates by movements of a lever to drive the motions of a cursor on a graphical screen — up, down, left, and right.

K, Kilo For our purposes, 1000. In "computerese" usually means 1024 (2^{10} — the closest number to the decimal number "1000" in the **binary** system).

Kb, Kbyte One "thousand" bytes. See **K, Kilo.**

Keypunch A keyboard device for producing cards with punched holes.

Light Pen A small pen-like **input device** used to point out choices, to draw lines, etc., on a **cathode ray tube.** Electronics associated with the light pen enable the computer to determine the position on the screen at which it is being pointed.

Line Printer A fairly high-speed impact **hard-copy output device.** Line printers usually use a rapidly rotating chain containing several copies of their **character** set. Multiple hammers, one in each print position, strike the chain at the time when desired characters are in position. Thus, when the chain is appropriately aligned, multiple characters of any given line are printed simultaneously. This printing process is much faster than hard copy **terminals** that print only one character at a time.

Location The place in or on a **storage device** where a single piece of data or a single **instruction** is stored.

Machine Language The **instructions** of a **computer system.** These are usually **binary** numbers and are idiosyncratic to any given type of computer.

Macro The name given to a **routine** written in **assembler** and utilized as a unit by the assembly-language **programmer,** who usually uses symbols to invoke the routine.

Magnetic-Ink Computer-Readable (MICR) A special **character** font printed with magnetic ink. This is the well-known character set often used by artists to depict "computer printing." It was first used for processing checks in banks; such characters are still frequently seen on checks, although more human-readable **optical character recognition** fonts have replaced MICR characters in most other applications.

Magnetic Memory Any memory device using magnetic fields as a means for storing data.

Magnetic Strip Card A small card resembling a credit card to which a strip of magnetizable material is affixed. Data can be read from or written onto this magnetic strip. An example of a common application for these cards is the subway system in Washington, D.C. In medicine, these cards are useful for containing identification and/or clinical information on ambulatory patients.

Management Consultant   A person involved in advising administrators, especially regarding organizational matters. Consultants are becoming increasingly involved in data processing and its impact on the organizations that use it.

Mass Storage Device   A **secondary memory device** holding large amounts of data.

Maxicomputer   Those computers most commonly found in large computer centers, typically with prices in the million-dollar range, e.g., IBM's model 370/158 or 370/168.

Mb (Megabyte)   One million **bytes**. 1000 **Kb**.

Mean Time Between Failures (MTBF)   The average length of time that will elapse between successive failures of any device.

Mean Time to Repair (MTTR)   The average amount of time it takes to restore a failed device to functioning status.

Medium   Any carrier on which data may be recorded, e.g., paper, disks, tapes, paper tape, **punched cards**. Plural: media.

Memory Size   The total amount of memory of a given type (such as **internal memory**) in a **computer system**.

Microcomputer   This term usually refers to a complete **computer system** built around a **microprocessor** CPU.

Microprocessor   Usually refers to a **central processing unit** formed on a single integrated circuit chip, though sometimes a few chips are used. Early microprocessors had eight-**bit words**, though some now have 16-bit words, making them virtually miniprocessors-on-a-chip.

Midicomputer   Colloquial term sometimes used to describe computers in the fuzzy zone between large **minicomputers** and small **maxicomputers**, e.g., Digital Equipment's PDP 11/70 and DEC system 20; Hewlett-Packard's HP3000; Interdata 7/32.

Minicomputer   An imprecise term usually referring to computers of moderate price (< \$500,000), e.g., Digital Equipment's PDP 11/34, Data General's Nova 3, or Hewlett-Packard's 21MX. Most have 16-**bit words**. It is increasingly difficult to make a meaningful distinction between the upper limit of minicomputers and the lower limit of **maxicomputers**, or between the lower limit of minicomputers and the upper limit of **microcomputers**.

Modem   A device for changing serial **binary** numbers into a signal that can be transmitted over standard telephone lines, or the reverse. Derived from words **MO**dulate/**DEM**odulate. Synonym: *dataset.*

Multiplexer A device for mixing data coming from or going to low-speed devices and sending it along one high-speed line, or the reverse. Example: a linkage between two cities handles 240 **characters**/second, and **terminals** are capable of printing 30 characters/second. Therefore communications from eight such terminals can be mixed (usually by interdigitation in time, i.e., time division multiplexing) by a multiplexer and sent along the one 240-character/second line. A demultiplexer is used to obtain the eight original independent character references. Also refers to the device on a **computer system** into which terminals plug and which passes the data from many terminals onto the computer's input/output channel.

Multistream Batch Operating System For an adequately detailed explanation, refer to Chapter 9.

Network An intercommunicating group of **computer systems** and/or **terminals.**

Node One of the computers or **terminals** in a **network.**

Object Code See below.

Object Program (Object Code) The code resulting from the compilation process. (See **compiler.**)

Off-Line Not directly computer-accessible. In the case of a **drive,** not attached to the computer. In the case of **media,** not mounted on a drive.

On-Line Opposite of **off-line.** An on-line application is one in which the user is directly dealing with a computer. Contrasted usually with **batch** processing, in which data is collected now and processed later.

Operating System The main system **programs** that provide methods of accessing system **resources** and that schedule **access** to those resources. The operating system often provides other services such as specific programs called "utilities" for **backup,** *accounting security,* etc. Synonyms: *supervisor, executive, monitor.* Often abbreviated OS.

Operator A person who performs functions needed during normal system utilization, such as feeding in cards, changing tapes or disks, initiating special **programs,** handling paper for the printing facilities, etc.

Optical Character Recognition (OCR) An OCR reader is a device for scanning and recognizing printed **characters** and transforming these into computer-readable form.

Optical Mark Recognition (OMR) An OMR reader senses the position of pencil marks on a card or a form, thereby providing a means of inputting multiple-choice data to a computer.

Optimizing Compiler A **compiler** that attempts to correct inefficiencies in the logic of **programs** in order to improve **execution** times, **internal memory** requirements, etc.

Output Device A machine for transforming data coming from the computer into a form readable by people or readable by other machines. In the latter sense, a storage **medium** like tape could be considered to be an output medium under some circumstances.

Paper Tape A continuous thin paper **medium,** usually about an inch wide, on which data is recorded as round punched holes. Once created, the paper tape cannot be altered. In most applications, this medium for storing data has become obsolete.

Parallel Interface A method of transmitting data a whole **word** or **byte** at a time from device to device, where a separate line is assigned to each **bit** being transferred in order to achieve a high rate of data transfer.

Patchboard An electrical panel that allowed the plugging in of wires to interconnect circuits in historical computers that used such a method of programming.

Peripheral Device Any **hardware** device other than the **central processing unit. Input, output,** or **storage device.**

Phoneme A quantum of sound with given frequency, timing, etc., characteristics that, when concatenated with other such quanta of different characteristics, can be used to generate a reasonable facsimile of human speech.

Plotter A device for producing graphical **hard copy** in which lines, curves, and **characters** are produced by moving a pen according to coordinates supplied by a computer. It can work in a "pen up" mode for moving without drawing and a "pen down" mode for drawing dots or continuous lines.

Polling The process whereby a computer indicates to a **terminal** that holds data that the terminal can transmit its data to the computer.

Printer-Plotter Typically refers to an electrostatic **output device** (working in a way similar to a Xerox copier) that is capable of producing both **characters** (for text) and graphical output. These devices are also available for producing characters only or for graphic output only.

Processing Manipulation of data. Performing **(executing)** computations.

Processor See **central processing unit.**

Program A list of instructions written in some **programming language** that controls what a computer will do. For example, a series of arithmetic commands (such as A+B÷C) tells the computer which calculations to perform on a specific set of variables.

Programmer The person who creates logical and error-free lists of **instructions** in a **programming language** for the solution of a problem. Some programmers are also responsible for definition of the **program** itself. (See **programmer/analyst.**)

Programmer/Analyst A person who performs the combined functions of a **programmer** and a **systems analyst.**

Programming Language (language) A set of **instructions** or symbols, and syntactical rules for using and combining them, for the writing of **programs.** There is a continuous evolution of high-level programming languages toward the point where the instruction **(words)** and the syntax (grammar) are as close to natural language as possible.

Project Manager A person who takes responsibility for the enforcement of the goals of a project. For instance, he/she ensures that appropriate work is performed by **programmers,** that schedules are met, that appropriate communication occurs between developers and users, and that a project stays within its budget.

Pseudo-Random Access Memory Memory in which it is possible to skip over most, but not all, **locations** in order to **access** any one desired location. For example, disks are said to be "pseudo-random access devices" since one can skip rapidly to the desired **track.** It is then necessary to wait until data on that track moves sequentially into place for reading.

Punched Card Commonly referred to as the "I.B.M." card." Patterns of rectangular holes, aligned in columns, can print up to 80 **characters** of information on a single card. Once created, a punched card cannot be modified, unless more information is added in previously unused columns.

Query Language A set of commands employed by a user to extract from a database data that meets specified criteria.

RAM, Random Access Memory A kind of **internal memory** whose **locations** can be **accessed** and the contents retrieved with the same access time for all locations. Usually refers to electronic (as opposed to magnetic) internal memory.

Read To retrieve data or an **instruction** from some storage **location** or **medium.**

Register A temporary electronic storage location in which **instructions** or data are placed while being subject to some arithmetic or other operation. Usually a register has the same **bit** length as a standard computer **word.**

Remote Job Entry (RJE) A process for permitting batch input of **programs** and/or data to a **computer system** in situations in which the user is distant from the computer. Data or programs to be transmitted are assembled into messages following one or another industry-standard format and are transmitted according to a standard protocol. Usually methods are employed for detecting errors and initiating retransmission when errors are detected. Ordinarily, at least a small **processor** and local **storage devices** (**internal memory** and/or small **secondary memory devices**) are employed to optimally use the long-distance communications link. Data is transmitted at speeds exceeding 2400 BPS via **modems.**

Resources Any hardware or software capabilities offered by a **computer system.** For example, file management problems, the central processing unit, and the line printer are all resources. The major concerns with resources are that they be available and that they be utilized as completely as possible so that one can get the maximum amount of work out of them.

ROM, Read Only Memory Memory from which it is possible to **read** information but onto which data cannot be **written.**

Routine A self-contained collection of **program** statements that perform some very specific subsection of an overall program. The same routine may be invoked numerous times within the same program. Thus it is useful to separate routines from the main body of a program, so that routines can be invoked many times without the necessity of repeating their statements many times.

Secondary Memory Device Those devices (excluding **internal memory**) that are used for storage of **programs** and data. One can usually **write** data onto these devices and **read** from them, although some secondary memory devices are read-only.

Semiconductor Memory Electronic memory whose individual memory cells (each storing a **binary bit**) are made up of transistor-like devices.

Sense Light A light whose on-off status is controlled by a **program.** There are also *sense switches,* switches whose on-off status can be **read** by a program.

Sequential Access Memory Memory devices such as tape on which, in order to **read** or **write** data at a specific **location,** all data intervening between that location and the current position must be read or passed over. Thus the more data to be passed over, the longer it takes to get to the data of interest.

Serial Interface An **input** or **output device** for a **computer system** that effects data transmission or reception. For output it transforms **parallel** data into a sequential train of pulses. For input it transforms data from a sequential train of pulses into parallel **binary words.**

Smart Terminal See **intelligent terminal.**

Software The **programs** that cause the computer to perform specific functions.

Software Engineering A relatively new field that addresses the efficient development of reliable and error-free **software.**

Software Maintenance The ongoing process of detecting and removing errors from existing **programs.** Commercially, this usually refers to the process of the manufacturer's supplying and installing new versions or corrections to old versions of **software** products such as **operating systems, programming languages,** and **applications packages.**

Software Package Usually refers to an **applications package,** but could refer to all the **software** in a **computer system.**

Software Transportability The ability to take a **program** written and working on one computer and to run it without modification on a different computer.

Source Code The **program** in its original **programming language,** before it is translated into **machine language.**

Storage Device See **secondary memory device.**

Stored Program Refers to the concept in which **instructions** are kept in **internal memory** for **execution** in the same form that data is kept. A **program** can be designed to alter itself as required when stored in this way.

Structured Programming An attempt to achieve better organization of **programs** and better program **documentation** in order to make programs more understandable, more error-free, and more efficient. This also involves the stepwise refinement of the problem itself, until a stage is reached where there is a simple correspondence between the logic of the program solution and the **instructions** or **routines** available in some **programming language.**

Supercomputer This designation usually refers to the most powerful computers. Such computers are normally capable of **executing** many million instructions per second and often have specialized **hardware** for calculating, **processing** arrays of numbers, handling large volumes of input and output, and speeding up processing. They are extremely expensive and are used only for the most complex computations.

Synchronous *Synchronous transmission* occurs according to a fixed time standard. In the case of synchronous communications, each **bit** transmitted as part of a message is expected at the receiving end within a fixed, limited time interval. A continuous string of **characters** is sent, with no blanks except between messages. See Fig. 6.3.

Systems Analyst (analyst) In general, a person responsible for the first attempts at stepwise refinement of a problem. He or she defines a problem in data processing terms and may indicate to **programmers** the directions for specific data processing solutions.

Systems House A company that develops **hardware** and/or **software** systems to user requirements.

Task Any procedure or set of procedures that must be performed by a computer, e.g., in **executing** a user's **program** (in which case the program is the task) or executing some portion of a program.

Tb (Terabyte) A trillion **bytes.** 1000 **Gb.**

Teletype An old-fashioned **input** and **output device,** used for creating **hard copy** output at low speed.

Terminal Any device for providing input and/or output to and/or from a computer.

Testing The process of subjecting a **program** to the conditions under which it must normally function in order to see if it works correctly.

Time-Sharing Operating System The section entitled "time-driven operating systems" in Chapter 9 explains this topic in sufficient depth.

Track A term that applies to magnetic storage **media** — disk or tape. Refers to the area that can be magnetized by a magnetic recording head. On a tape **drive** there are normally seven or nine heads that record seven or nine linear tracks on the tape. This is the same idea as the multitrack cassettes for music. On a spinning disk, a single track is a circle. There are several hundred concentric circular tracks on a disk; the one on the outer run is the longest track, while the one closest to the spindle is the shortest. However, all can contain the same number of pieces of data.

Trackball Similar to a **joystick,** but uses a ball moved by the palm of the hand of a human operator instead of a lever held by the fingers.

Transaction Logging The process of redundantly recording everything that users input to a computer. Used in conjunction with a backup copy of system data for restoring data stored on the **computer system** to its original condition in cases in which database is inadvertently destroyed.

Turnaround Time Can be measured in many ways, but nominally is the elapsed time from submission of a job to a **computer system** until all output has been produced.

Turnkey System A **computer system** marketed as a complete product, meeting specified needs of a given spectrum of users.

Unbundled Refers to the fact that the cost of the **software** is not included with the cost of the **hardware** in the overall price of a **computer system.** (Cf. **bundled.**)

Up; Up-Time The period of time during which the computer is functioning normally.

Wand   An **input device** used to read optical **bar code** labels by sensing the optical pattern of the light and dark areas.

Word   The number of **bits** processed as a single unit in an arithmetic operation.

Write   To record data on a memory device.

X-Y Digitizer   An **input device** that allows the motion of a pen or cursor to be transduced and fed to the computer as a series of X-Y coordinates.

INDEX